C000121466

Surfacing

Surfacing

PEOPLE COPING WITH DEPRESSION
AND MENTAL ILLNESS

Marion Scher

BOOK**STORM**

This book was made possible through generous support by Cipla South Africa.

Cipla

© Marion Scher, 2021

All rights reserved. No part of this book may be reproduced or transmitted in any form or by any means, electronic or mechanical, including photocopying, recording or any information storage or retrieval system, without permission from the copyright holder.

ISBN: 978-1-928257-88-2
e-ISBN: 978-1-928257-89-9

First edition, first impression 2021

Published by Bookstorm (Pty) Ltd
PO Box 4532
Northcliff 2115
Johannesburg
South Africa
www.bookstorm.co.za

Edited by Angela Voges
Proofread by Tracey Hawthorne
Author photograph by Jason Crouse
Cover image by iStock/Hailshadow
Cover design by mr design
Book design and typesetting by Triple M Design
Printed in the USA

For Zane Wilson and SADAG,
without whom South African mental health would be far poorer.

Contents

Foreword ix

Introduction 1
1 Diane Naidoo: A daughter's suicide 5
2 Melissa du Preez: Depression 28
3 Daryl Brown: A suicide attempt 44
4 Sindi van Zyl: Depression 68
5 Sipho Simelane: Suicide attempts 90
6 Dobson de Beer Procter: Depression 112
7 Alexandra Wallis: Postnatal depression 139
8 AJ Venter: Anxiety disorder 162
9 Yvette Hess: Bipolar disorder 174
10 Zane Wilson: Panic disorder 197
11 Charlene Sunkel: Schizophrenia 209

Acknowledgements 231

Foreword

According to the World Health Organization (WHO), South
Africa has the sixth highest rate of suicide in Africa, with the
data revealing approximately 12 of every 100 000 people in the
country completing suicide.[1] It is commonly accepted that the
majority of suicides and suicide attempts occur among individuals who suffer from undiagnosed and untreated depression,
with the WHO estimating that more than 300 million people
are affected by depression worldwide.[2]

Considering these concerning statistics, about two years ago
Cipla started an educational campaign to create widespread
awareness about the importance of mental health. We also
wanted to emphasise that depression is in fact a medical condition, and that mental health is equally important as physical
health. Just as any other organ in the body can become ill or
affected, so too can the brain. We wanted people to know that
it's okay not to be okay.

In line with our ethos of 'caring for life' and as part of our
continued campaign to eradicate the stigma around mental
health, Cipla is proud to sponsor this book. We hope it will
start an honest and refreshing dialogue about mental health
so that people don't have to struggle in silence. As American

actress Glenn Close stated, mental health needs 'more sunlight, more candour, more unashamed conversation'.[3]

Depression does not simply go away, and there is no shame in seeking professional help for it. Whether you are helping a friend, or need help yourself, you can always call the Cipla SADAG 24-hour mental health helpline on 0800 456 789 or contact them via WhatsApp on 076 882 2775 between 9am and 5pm.

Paul Miller
CEO of Cipla South Africa

1. World Health Organization (WHO). World Health Statistics data visualizations dashboard. (2016). Available at: http://apps.who.int/gho/data/node.sdg.3-4-viz-2?lang=en
2. World Health Organization. Depression. 1–4 (2015). http://www.who.int/news-room/fact-sheets/detail/depression
3. Close, G. 'Mental Illness: The Stigma of Silence' in HuffPost Contributor (17 November 2011). Available at https://www.huffpost.com/entry/mental-illness-the-stigma_b_328591

Introduction

Writing this book has been overwhelming at times. After all, the people in these pages have put their trust in me to tell their immensely personal, often raw stories with one common theme – to help break the stigma of mental illness and to show there's hope with every story.

The truth is we all have mental health, just like we have physical health. Not everyone will experience mental illness, but everyone will have certain times when they struggle with their mental well-being.

Many years ago I was writing for a men's magazine and suggested to the editor that we do a story on men and depression. His answer was that such a story 'would depress his readers'. Well, I promise you definitely won't feel depressed after reading these amazing people's stories. You'll come away feeling inspired, and whether you see your own story here or that of a friend or family member, you'll most importantly be armed with the knowledge and understanding to help them. You'll shed a tear or two but, surprisingly with this topic, you'll also laugh along the way.

Each chapter tells a completely different type of story with one common thread – how each one learnt how to deal with

1

their illness, conquering their own personal mountain and going on to lead healthy, fulfilled lives – better lives than they'd ever hoped to lead.

This may be the first time many readers really get to understand the difference between depression, bipolar disorder and schizophrenia. Sadly, there is also a mother's story of losing her daughter to suicide but uses this experience to try to stop other families from suffering the same fate.

My journey with mental health, unlike that of many of the people featured in this book, didn't involve personal experience. In fact, had anyone come to me before 1996 and told me they were feeling depressed, my answer would have been that I'd take them out for a drink or lunch, or maybe recommend a few days away at the coast or in the bush. Like most people, I had no idea then that depression was a real illness and that the last thing a person living with mental illness wants to hear is to 'snap out of it'.

This all changed for me 26 years ago after meeting and interviewing Zane Wilson, founder and CEO of the South African Depression and Anxiety Group (SADAG) for a Q and A column I wrote for *Cosmopolitan* magazine. She told me about her ten-year journey to hell and back before being diagnosed with panic disorder. Sitting with this vivacious, well-groomed woman all those years ago in her lovely home in the suburbs of Sandton, I thought, *How could she be someone who lives with mental illness? She looks so normal, so healthy and full of life.* This was where my learning started, and it's what I've tried to get across in this book: what you see on the outside isn't always what's going on inside.

Zane, with her marketing background, knew exactly how to work with the media and soon started sending me story ideas about mental health, together with case studies and recommendations for mental health professionals to interview.

Since then I've written and learnt about bipolar disorder, borderline personality disorder, generalised anxiety disorder, schizophrenia and many more mental health conditions. What I found was that, whether these were published in *Fairlady*, *Longevity*, *True Love*, *Marie Claire* or the *Saturday Star*, they had one thing in common – the feedback from readers thanking me for highlighting their story and illness, one they felt they'd had to hide. Mental health shouldn't be a secret.

At the end of each chapter there's a toolbox, written about that particular story, which will give you further insight into the specific mental illness and tips on dealing with that issue – not just for the person going through this, but also for family and friends.

There were two things I never expected when I went to interview the inimitable Zane Wilson all those years ago: first, that I would go on to write so much about mental health; and second, that with my now-dear friend Zane and the wonderful Cassey Chambers, Operational Director at SADAG, and her amazing team, I'd be involved not just in writing about mental health but in working with hundreds of other journalists and editors to help them understand mental illness and help spread the word.

This book will hopefully inform – and, more importantly, inspire – you to reach out and offer help and encouragement to anyone you feel might be battling secret demons or simply needing a kind word.

This book is my small contribution to knocking down the walls surrounding mental illness and helping people tell their stories. Everyone in this book was brave enough to let me use their real names. For this I want to thank them, and for their time and patience in working with me.

Marion Scher

1

DIANE NAIDOO

A daughter's suicide

There are those among us who are blessed with the power
to save what is loved by another. But powerless to use
this blessing for love themselves.
– Alicia Keys, 'Try Sleeping with a Broken Heart'

I've heard about Diane Naidoo – a wonderful, brave mother who'd lost her teenage daughter to suicide – through SADAG, as she's volunteered in different capacities for them. But I've never met her. She suggests that we meet for the interview at her office at Nedbank in Newtown, Johannesburg, where she works as a resource planner for Nedbank's call centres.

I've interviewed parents who have lost children to suicide before, and I always make sure I have my journalistic condom firmly on, as these are never easy interviews. I arrive at the bank and wait for Diane at reception. As the lift opens I immediately spot her – she comes rushing towards me with arms wide open. *This,* I think, *is a woman who is comfortable with herself and where she is, and not someone who has lost herself in grief.* We go up to the impressive company dining area and sit at a quiet corner table.

The first thing Diane does as we sit down is take out her

phone and show me a photo of her beautiful 15-year-old daughter, Tenniel. She looks at it lovingly, and I realise that it is a photo frozen in time: Diane won't get to see her grow into an adult, or be there for her 21st birthday, her wedding, or any other momentous event in a young woman's life, because on 27 May 2012 Tenniel took her own life.

Just three years later, Diane lost her beloved husband Neelan, her childhood sweetheart – this would be more than most people could take. But I sense a strong resilience in Diane and know she's learning how to live through this.

She's happy to talk to me – or, as she puts it, to take me on her journey of love, sorrow and pain. She feels strongly that she wants to help others cope with tragic circumstances, using her personal experience and how she's almost recovered and moved into a more positive place. Today, with most of her husband's family having also passed on, she shares her life with her 16-year-old daughter Tiyaana.

'This photo is important to me because Tenniel told me, "Mom, that picture is going to be very famous one day." I asked her why but didn't get an answer. Today, looking back, it's obvious. She knew then she was going to take her own life. All the classic signs were there, but I didn't know or recognise them. That's why telling her story is so important to me. If I can spare just one family the pain of going through what we've been through, it will be worth it.' I can see that this is a cry from Diane's heart, one she wants to make as loudly as she can.

The eldest of seven siblings, Diane was born in Lenasia, which she still calls home. 'I was very happy growing up in a large family of seven children and at 22 married the love of my life, Neelan. By 23 I was a mother to my first daughter Tenniel – a perfect, gorgeous baby. The advantage of being surrounded by such a large family was the support structure, particularly on my husband's side. Like me, he also came from a large family, where he was the youngest. When I fell pregnant with Tenniel there was great excitement as there hadn't been a baby in their family for 12 years. My mother-in-law saw it as her baby having a baby, and the whole event was joyful.

'Our marriage was a good one, with occasional challenges – like most people have. Funnily enough, when Tenniel was born a lot of great things happened to me and I particularly grew as a woman. I was working for Nedbank as a call agent then and over the years moved up in the company, first to become a team leader and then, through my amazing mentor Dawie van der Merwe, to where I am today – a resource planner, helping to build contact centres and develop systems,' she explains proudly.

I can see by the way her colleagues greet her as they pass our table that she's well-liked and respected, and is 100 per cent committed to the job that has given her so much. Her boss Dawie arrives in the dining area and she calls him over to meet me, explaining about the interview and book. He tells me he's always been fully supportive of Diane's work in mental health, as he knows the importance of this. When he leaves, Diane continues with her story.

'Tenniel went from a bubbly, happy baby to a vibrant, inquisitive child, although this curiousity led to her asking questions that perhaps I should have paid more attention to, particularly around death. When she was very small she had a little bird that died. As many parents do, we made a big fuss around its burial, making a small cross with its name on it, and held a service in the garden. We supported her and grieved with her, patting our eyes to match her tears. Anything around

7

death and heaven aroused an unusual response in her and the questions would be endless.

'Other than that, she grew up like any other normal kid. She was highly intelligent and cheeky with it. She took after me and was very feisty, with a strong character, which sometimes saw her knocking heads with her father, who was the soft one. When it came to the two of us, somehow we never challenged each other. We'd know just when to draw the line. But when Tenniel turned 13 we noticed she suddenly started having mood swings. We put this down to normal teenage behaviour, with the hormones kicking in. Now, comparing her to my younger daughter Tiyaana, who's 13, I can pick up a big difference in behaviour.

'Growing up, Tenniel had no fears – until one day she did. Suddenly, when she couldn't deal with something she'd start going to a little corner on her own. The feisty child was disappearing to be replaced by a quiet, moody one. I still thought this was normal. Where today my younger daughter Tiyaana would just say to me, "Mom, I'd like to be left alone for a few minutes," Tenniel would disappear into this deep space. At its worst she'd say to me, "Mom, I don't want to live. Surely there's something more beyond this life?" I'd ask her why she was saying this. I'd point out that she was the most popular girl in school, with a trail of followers. She was an attracter, not a rejecter. She was never bullied. I'd ask her why she'd say this to which she'd reply, "I just feel like I don't want to live." This was all during her thirteenth year, and alarm bells should have gone off in my head right then. But family would say, "Ah, she'll get over it. It's just a period in her life. She's a teenager, let her scream and go to her room."

'Having said this, she wasn't a difficult teenager but if I'd known the signs then that scream suicide today, I would have done things differently. I would have said, "I have a problem with my daughter," and sought help. But how could I know? Like most parents it wasn't something I was educated on. You learn your life lessons from your family but my mom, my sisters and brothers – no one picked up anything they felt unusual with her.'

Dealing with teenage children, particularly girls, can be challenging at the best of times, so where is the line between 'difficult' and 'we have a problem'? This is where parents need to put their own fears of what they might hear aside and consult mental health professionals – something Diane wants as many people to know as possible.

Diane has severe rheumatoid arthritis and in March 2012 she was on a sabbatical from work for treatment. She explains how Tenniel was home that day as there was no water at school. At lunchtime, Diane asked Tenniel to fetch her little sister from school and when they arrived back all seemed to be fine.

'After my treatments I couldn't walk properly and was lying on the bed. I said to the girls that as their dad was about to come home they should just tidy up a bit. At this, Tenniel gave me a strange look and screamed at me, "Do as you please." That day, she was in a darker place than I'd probably ever seen her. At that time her moods were like a yo-yo, happy one minute and down the next, with some aggression thrown in.' Diane's voice tightens as she goes on. This story never gets easier in the telling.

'When her dad arrived home, Tiyaana ran up to him and said her sister had just shouted at mommy. We have a very long passage in our house and I heard Tenniel calling me from the end of the passage, saying, "Come here." I started walking towards her, saying, "I won't tell Dad you shouted." Her reply was to say, "Let me show you what I can do." And right there she took a blade and slashed her wrists in front of me, then squeezed her arm so the blood spurted out. This was aggression and anger and I didn't know where it came from. Had this been building up to something this extreme? At first I found myself rooted to the floor. As it was I was battling to walk, so I just screamed for my husband to come and see what Tenniel had done. He was bewildered and wanted to know where the blood had come from. Only a few minutes before, when he'd arrived home, Tenniel had seemed fine to him. Now he was stunned at what was in front of him.' The shock of this moment still shows on Diane's face.

'She screamed at us to stay away from her when we said we needed to rush her to the hospital. She insisted the only person she'd let near her was her uncle, my brother. He came rushing from his home three roads away and all this time she still wouldn't let us near her. She put herself on our dining room table and put a bloodied hand down and made designs on the table top with her blood. It looked almost satanic at the time. My mind was racing as all I wanted was to get her to the hospital. I was in a state of panic.

'My brother took her to the hospital and we raced behind him. Even in the hospital, at first she refused to see us. The bleeding was so bad that she had to have emergency surgery to stitch her up. Eventually she saw a counsellor but it was three days before she saw a psychiatrist and even then she just had one session with her. She called us and said she wanted Tenniel to heal physically from her wounds before treating her further. So we took her home and kept her in bed, spoiling her with treats and trying to meet her every need. Tenniel, though, never said she was sorry or even why she did it. Her father asked her what could he buy her to make her feel better and she said Winnie the Pooh, her favourite childhood character, and he rushed out to find one. I remember thinking at the time that it appeared she enjoyed the pain and I couldn't understand why.'

This was a classic case of mishandling by the hospital whose staff didn't think this was serious enough for further mental health assessment. For them, it was just another case of an angry teen, but correct direction to a psychiatrist could have saved a life.

'Once her arms started to heal she seemed like the old Tenniel again and everything appeared to be fine. What we didn't know at the time was that for the last two years she'd had a boyfriend, who was two years older than her. We're not sure but possibly the reason we hadn't met him before was because he was older than her, we don't really know. She wasn't normally secretive but did like to control things in her own way. We finally met him on 30 April 2012 and the very next day he was killed in a car accident – possibly the catalyst that saw Tenniel, just 27 days later, take her own life.'

Diane pauses here, perhaps drawing the strength it takes to continue with her harrowing story.

'The night of this accident Neelan and I had decided to go out for dinner and without knowing it we passed the accident, obviously not knowing it was him. Tenniel was at home with her granny and we'd left instructions that her phone was to be switched off at a certain time. Her boyfriend had been a passenger in the car and when the accident happened he'd furiously tried to message Tenniel to tell her how much he loved her, hoping to hear back.

'It was only the next morning we received a message to say he'd been involved in an accident and had been asking for Tenniel while lying in intensive care. She then turned her phone on to find a flood of messages, those days on Mxit. This was sheer hell for her and for us. We did everything in our power to comfort her but when I look back now I realise she had then set the date for her own death – Thursday 28 May. The last day she'd been with her boyfriend was a Thursday, so I think this was significant to her. The Thursday before this, Tiyaana had a speech competition, which I think ruled out that day as she didn't want to spoil something that meant so much to her little sister. The 17th of May had been Tiyaana's birthday and we'd had a family dinner. I'd asked Tenniel to get Tiyaana into the bath and dressed before everyone arrived for dinner. Tiyaana later told me Tenniel had said to her that if it wasn't her birthday she'd have been in heaven.'

When you speak to family members, particularly those of young people who have taken their own lives, you often hear these subtle and not-so-subtle messages. It's knowing when to take them seriously that's the hard part, as Diane found out.

'Only later I realised all the warning signs were there. On the Monday before taking her life she'd asked us to cut her hair – a strange thing for her to do as she had gorgeous long hair she was so proud of. When one of her friends asked why she'd cut her hair she replied, "Where I'm going I need to look beautiful." The day before her death she went to each friend saying, "Goodbye, I love you, please remember that." She said to one friend she knew had depression, "Remember, if you don't love yourself, do something about it. If you're not happy about yourself, do something about it." I didn't know what that meant at the time. Now I do.'

Diane and Neelan only found this out after Tenniel passed. She'd started giving her things away that week and suddenly starting eating sweets – something she never did. 'The morning before her death she also gave herself a full facial, a manicure, and did her eyebrows,' Diane recalls, gently shaking her head, almost in disbelief.

Diane asks me if I'm an Alicia Keys fan, which I am, and then tells me how much Tenniel loved her and the significance of one particular song for her. She tells me that the rather dark song and video 'Try Sleeping with a Broken Heart' was one of Tenniel's favourites. The main lyric in the song is 'I am going to try and find a way to make it without you', with the video showing her touching a puppy which is lying down, supposedly dead, but which, after she lays her hand on it, comes alive. There was obviously deep significance for Tenniel here.

'Two days prior to her passing she brought home this little puppy which she gave to her dad, saying, "I bought a gift for you and Mom." We asked where she found the puppy and she said the puppy was given to her by a friend. She asked if we could keep her and call her Pepper. Neelan said we can't afford another dog but she begged and we gave in.

'The night before her death she lay on the couch in a foetal position, very quietly, with the dog. I was lying down in my room with Tiyaana, who was only five years old at the time. I thought about Tenniel possibly showing signs of depression but thought we were working through it. We were giving her extra pampering and buying her little gifts. That night I received a call telling me my cousin had passed away from rheumatoid arthritis, the same condition I have, and so the next morning my sister came to pick me up to take me to my aunt's house. When she arrived Tenniel handed her a present, a new

13

jersey I'd only bought her the week before. She handed it to her telling her she loved her. That was her goodbye to her aunt.' Again, Diane didn't pick up the signs.

'Before my sister arrived I'd showered and was sitting on my bed when Tenniel came to sit next to me. She took my hand, looked at my fingers and said, "Promise me you'll take care of yourself," and I'm thinking, *I'm not going to die like my cousin died from this.* She was wise enough to play me. I'm thinking she's now talking about my cousin but it was her way of saying goodbye to me. Her way of saying, Mom, take care. I got dressed and, after kissing her, left. She called me back and said, Mom, please come back here. I went back and she said, "I just need you to know that I love you," and I said, "I love you too, I'll always love you." And without realising it that was our last conversation.' Our interview stops for a while as Diane takes a drink and a deep breath before continuing.

'She waited until no one was at home and then, using her school tie, she hanged herself. Again, if only I'd known the relevance when, after washing the tie two weeks prior, she said, "I'm going to use that tie." I thought she meant for school but I later found out she knew it was almost unbreakable.

'She knew exactly how to tie the knot and her neck was broken instantly. She'd planned everything, the day and time. Based on the Alicia Keys video she even died holding the puppy in her arms. She played out the video in her own death. She was found by our domestic worker and her granny and my same brother who rushed her to the hospital was once again summoned to then what became a crime scene.'

Diane was at her aunt's house when this happened. Her brother called her sister and Diane knew something was very wrong just by the expression on her face. 'She said to me, "Di, we need to go *now*." I still had no inkling of what was happening. I asked what's wrong and she replied that Tenniel wasn't well and we had to go home. Before we reached home we were told to go to the hospital so I thought she must have fallen and broken something. At the hospital, my mom, brother and Neelan's sister were with her. I knew this hospital as it was where I had my treatments, so the first thing I did on arriving was to look for my medical aid card. My family were all saying, "No, just go." As I walked in the doctor came up to me and took my hand. The whole hospital knew me from my time there, and Tenniel – particularly because she was the girl who captured your heart, with her captivating eyes alone. When I saw her lying there wrapped up in a blanket I still didn't realise what had happened. To me she looked normal, like she was sleeping. Suddenly I heard the words "time of death". "What are you talking about?" I wanted to know. "Look at her lying there – she's so perfect." Then I had to wait for Neelan to come from work. When they'd called him to say come to the hospital he'd responded by saying, "Please don't tell me my wife is sick." They said, "No, Tenniel's not well."'

I reach for her hand to comfort her as she finishes this part of the story. Without saying anything, we sit for a few moments before she carries on. When you cover stories like this it's always hard to know what to say. Even though it's been ten years since Diane's tragic loss, the pain feels fresh.

'It was and still is, to an extent, all a blur. People came in and out all the time, my boss, colleagues, friends and family. It had a massive impact, not just at Tenniel's school but all the local high schools. That day when we got home from the hospital we couldn't get into our house because there were so many kids surrounding it. Again I thought, *Tenniel, if you were so popular and so loved, why?* It just didn't make sense.'

Suicide rarely makes sense. It's not a case of that person's life being so bad – at least, not on the surface. But what makes that person find life so intolerable that each day is a challenge until they can't take another moment?

'At her funeral there were close to 600 people. *Where did they all come from?* I wondered. We're Catholic and normally when someone takes their own life they don't allow the body into the church. Tenniel, though, had gone to confession the Sunday before and so they accepted her body in the church. It wasn't a full Mass and she wasn't given the last rites. That last Sunday, as we left the church Tenniel had asked me, "When I get to heaven do you think St Peter will know my name?" I said, "Yes, St Peter will know your name." Again – another sign. She'd also recently asked me if someone took their own life and asked for forgiveness would God forgive them. I told her God forgives you for anything you ask forgiveness for, not knowing in my wildest dreams what she had in mind.

'We really didn't think this was a possibility and afterwards our first thoughts were to track what she'd been looking at online and on her phone, but she'd wiped everything clean and there were no clues.'

Every parent and family member will blame themselves, maybe not for the death, but for the fact that they hadn't done enough – or done anything – to stop it. Many cases show that, even if others are able to intervene at some level, the determination to do this often wins out. Using lies and manipulation, they assure you they're fine, and will find a way to end their lives.

'Although we did have incredible support from everyone, it was and still is a journey you take on your own. There's also the blame game. Neelan and I were in a world of pain and deep depression. And as much as we didn't want to, just beneath the surface there was blame. A few days after her funeral I even wanted to feel what she'd felt, so I took her tie and put it on. I didn't want to die – I just wanted to know what the experience felt like. I wanted to understand what went on in her mind.'

'We'd decided to tell Tiyaana that her sister was jumping on the bed and fell and broke her neck but we weren't to know then that a year and nine months later she'd be watching me on a talk show on national television telling the story of how her sister hanged herself. When I got home she was in a total frenzy over the fact that I'd lied to her. We knew the truth would come out, but we'd been hoping she would be older before she had to hear this.

'Neelan took a very different approach to the situation than me. He'd been through major trauma at 12 years old when he'd tragically lost his brother. He'd had counselling as a child and had developed a coping mechanism then, but this didn't work this time around. The death of your own child is a very different thing.

'In this time of deep mourning and grief, trying to deal with all the emotions of losing a child, Neelan and I went through some very difficult times, with our six-year-old daughter watching us. She'd often do random drawings of everything, and even invented an imaginary friend who obviously kept her sane.'

A child's suicide often puts the ultimate strain on a marriage and often sees its complete and irreparable breakdown, even of one as strong as the Naidoos'. They realised they needed help as their marriage and home life was in total darkness. Their once-balanced home, with a perfect family and in-laws right next to them, sharing family celebrations and holiday times, had suddenly come to an abrupt end.

'Neelan and I separated emotionally from each other. Although the love was there we'd become distant, both dealing with things in our own way. During this time we were visited by many of our community support groups, one being Compassionate Friends – an organisation that helps bereaved families. They knew our family so it was easy for them to offer their support, along with our church members, priest and Tenniel's friends, who were also grieving and who held on to us for support. For me, this was way too deep. It was as though I'd been divided into different puzzle pieces that no longer fitted, as the most important piece was missing. As much as I tried to fit the gaps it just wouldn't come together as complete. And although I appreciated all this support, it wasn't enough to conquer my pain and help me through this ordeal.

'After six months, I realised I needed to get professional help. Neelan resisted at first, saying he was fine, so I contacted a family friend, Gavin Frank, a highly respected psychologist from Lenasia, who was also a member of Compassionate Friends. I started opening up to him about my ups and downs, highs and lows. His personal experience equipped me with emotional healing and his therapy got me through my hell on earth. You're fighting a feeling that's beyond any explanation but he guided me in the process of grief and acceptance. From there I made choices that have taken me to where I am today. Tiyaana and Neelan eventually started therapy with him and also benefited greatly from his simple yet extremely effective methods.'

Seeking help gave Diane the tools to carry on, and she proudly tells me where this took her.

'I knew I needed to change my chain of actions, so I decided to channel the hurt, pain and sadness into a more positive light. One way I did this was to join SADAG, the most amazing, inspirational choice I took and where I'm still involved today, with live television chats, writing articles and more. The urge to tell my story just grew stronger as I wanted to share my experience with the world and help other kids not to do what Tenniel had. I wanted them to understand what it does to a family.

'During my deepest, saddest moments, I joined campaigns at local schools, creating awareness, talking to youth in churches, just wanting to save these kids. But if they make the choice and we as parents, family and friends don't see the signs, this is of no value. So every Mental Health Day and International Awareness of Teen Suicide Day I take a personal moment to ensure I add to the value of this cause helping to create awareness.'

Looking around her at her offices and colleagues, Diane explains how much her work means to her. 'Throughout my difficult journey Nedbank were amazing to me and I took a whole year off for which I was really grateful. They've always been incredibly supportive of the work I've done as a mental healthcare advocate.' She points to a boardroom behind us. 'They even allowed a *Carte Blanche* team in to film me there. When I went back to work I was really eager to get going again and immerse myself in work.'

Again, though, I see Diane brace herself as she goes on to tell me about the next horrific incident in her life. Just three years after Tenniel's death, the unimaginable happened – Neelan was killed in an accident, and again her life stood still. 'I sat down and said, "Lord, I have to ask you, what more? What next?" The next morning, I called SADAG without saying who

19

I was. I just needed to know how to deal with this. I'd lost my daughter and now my husband. They asked me how I'd lost my daughter which I skirted around. I said I just needed to know what to do. I remember one of our local doctors coming over and giving me some pills and I did sleep for a while.

'We had to wait for Neelan's sister to arrive from the United States, so there was four days before his burial. This was a daunting experience, knowing he was lying in that mortuary and not having closure with him. Then returning to the same gravesite where Tenniel was buried to bury him. This was a journey without comprehension. I sometimes sit back and think, *How did I do this? How?*

'This was really my third loss because I'd also lost a son who I gave birth to on Christmas day 2001 and who only survived for thirty minutes. Tenniel was desperately waiting for her little brother and we had to explain to her he wasn't coming. This possibly contributed to the way she thought. We'll never know.

'After my husband's death, I found myself slipping into my rabbit hole again – my safe place. I closed myself off to the world and started self-inflicting bad behaviours just to feel numb, like not eating, living on water. It's still a battle but seven years later I'm improving.

'Around this time I stopped my involvement with SADAG and kept myself busy, becoming deeply involved with my career, working long hours and only sleeping when my body could no longer hold on. I hid from the world, angry and bitter at anything that seemed good, and then I realised where I was heading … So, again, my challenge became to get out of the rabbit hole and start dealing with my life. SADAG was the way, and once again I made contact and became actively involved.'

It's people like Diane volunteering to share their stories that makes SADAG's work so much more effective. It's one thing to say watch your child for signs of suicide, but quite another when you hear a story such as this.

'When Neelan died, Tiyaana was only eight years old and had already suffered the loss of her sister. When I look at her I'm always amazed at her strength and the way she deals with things. We both still need therapy because we're still healing. In my family, Tenniel was my first death. I still have my 94-year-old granny and until my daughter I hadn't buried anyone in my life. This added to the force of the incident.'

Again, Diane pulls out her phone and smiles broadly as she shows me a photo of Tiyaana, now also a beautiful teenager with eyes full of passion and energy. Like any proud mother, Diane tells me more about her daughter, but this is not the usual brag.

'Through all the trauma Tiyaana's found her own coping mechanism. She draws a lot, expressing her emotions through art, particularly drawing girls. This strength doesn't stop me being overcautious with her, though. If she's in her room alone for more than five minutes and I can't hear anything I start calling her and I'll call and call. I think parents who have lost a child will understand this. Often parents will get so lost in their grief they forget to focus on their other kids also. Yes, this person has left you but the other one is still here and they're also going through a lot.

'Last year she was invited to visit family in Las Vegas. Although it wasn't easy, I knew I had to trust her and let her go. She must become her own person. I don't want what happened to Tenniel to happen to Tiyaana and at the same time I don't expect her to replace anything. I think as parents that's what we do. It's also not easy to talk about these things.

'My arthritis has led to me having some health problems

recently and I said to the doctor that the medications won't work if my mind isn't right. I felt myself slipping emotionally so I've gone back to my therapist, Gavin Frank. For the last two years I'd taken a break from working with SADAG as talking about suicide can take its toll, but being asked to participate in this book has renewed my desire to work in this field. I was particularly active in my community and also my church. I even managed to convince my priest that suicide isn't a sin,' she says with a sideways smile.

Dealing with yourself and family at these times is hard, but having to deal with judgemental friends and community members is a different ballgame. If you know someone who has gone through such an ordeal, think before you speak. At the same time, don't stay away if you don't know what to say. This is when even a brief comforting word or thought is really needed, and makes a big difference.

'Now I'm able to look back at the lessons I've learnt along the way. Your friends may judge you as a bad mother, or simply avoid you, not quite knowing what to say to you. The one thing I've learnt above all is that whether it's your child, friend, neighbour, cousin or a random person – if you see anyone who doesn't look normal to you, or is wearing a fake smile, is in their own zone, go and have a conversation with them on a light level. Gauge their feelings.'

As we're coming to the end of our interview, Diane wants me to promise to make sure people hear her story, which I assure her they will do.

'Another message I want to get out there for parents who have lost a child to suicide: don't just sit back and accept it, and don't keep it a secret. I won't accept this to be my journey – it's not about me. It's about the bigger journey and I want to see this journey grow. I want to see positivity here. I'm not going to save souls – that's not my intention. But if I can help just one person, then everything's worth it. I want to see changes, particularly in the field of mental health. I want to see the government become involved, individuals and whole communities getting involved. White, black, Indian, coloured – we all shy away from anything to do with mental health. It's easy to say I didn't see the signs, but they were there. We don't want to take the shame and blame, so we hide. But I'm not ashamed about this because I'm now the living reason to change things.'

Diane has a message for moms, too. 'You never stop grieving for the child you've lost. I'll always wonder what she'd look like in a wedding gown. What kind of 16-year-old she'd have been. You must watch out for the signs. Today's pressures are so intense it can happen in a split second and you can't undo it. That's the sad part of suicide. I believe in fate but I believe if you're wise enough and daring enough you're going to get it right. Tenniel did.'

And to teens, she has this to say: 'Every young girl should have their own lifeline, someone to confide in. This doesn't have to be their parents or a relative – just someone they trust enough to talk to. Communities need to know of lifelines like SADAG and we need to openly say to our children, particularly teen-agers, there's another channel you can reach out to. They need to understand it's strictly confidential, whether they've begun a sexual relationship, experimented with drugs, whatever the issue, there's someone to listen and help. At schools there's sex education but nothing about mental health awareness. I hope to be able to go into schools again and share my story.

'Suicide is not a culture and it's not a background. In my own Indian society, like most others, there's a stigma attached to suicide. My aim is to change this stigma within my own and other cultures. It mustn't stay a secret. It's something people would rather not talk about, but if we don't, how can we empower people? How can we make them understand that it's not about doing something after it happens, but before?

'When I first saw the signs to watch out for with teen suicide at SADAG I could have taken a gun right then and shot myself. The signs were all there – as clear as day, but I just didn't know. I do now, and there's no way I'm not going to teach others. It doesn't have to happen to other people's children.'

Of all the things that could happen to parents, siblings, family members and friends, the hardest to fathom is suicide. 'Because of my deep loss I ensure that death, anniversaries, birthdays and any special occasions of my family who are no longer with us are celebrated, crying and doing something special for them – offering a special Mass or writing an inspirational article in my personal diary. This contributes to my overall strength and gives me hope that someday I'll achieve recovery from my tragic journey.

'What was once deep pain and sadness I've turned into a positive light to make a difference in society and to inspire others that we can heal – but to do this, we need to accept it, feel it and deal with it.'

Tiyaana was only five when her big sister Tenniel took her life. But this meant a different kind of life for her growing up. 'I knew that my mom worried about me more than some of my other friends' parents but I mostly understood,' she says. 'There would be times when I'd ask my mom if I could go somewhere with my friends and she would be concerned, but it was never really a problem.

'I grew up understanding about mental health and that you

have to deal with it and talk about it. My way of dealing with things when they get too much for me is to lose myself in my drawing and writing, which I love to do. This really helps me get through tough days.

'At school they don't really deal with anything to do with mental health but I always talk to my friends and they know they can talk to me about their problems. I think today young people do talk more about mental health issues but there's still a stigma around it, which is a pity. I always want to encourage other kids my age to talk about their problems and get help if they need to.'

TOOLBOX TIPS

Normal teenage behaviour vs mental health issues

If you're not sure whether your teenager is just going through normal adolescence or is experiencing mental health difficulties, check.

❏ Rather have a professional tell you there's nothing to worry about than have regrets.
❏ Even in the normal ups and downs of adolescence, having a therapist that teenagers can speak to confidentially can be beneficial.

Notice significant changes in behaviour

Children change during adolescence, but not so significantly that their whole way of being changes. Watch out for:

❏ Differences in their interactions with parents, friends and teachers.

❏ Changes in their interests, things they enjoy or in their school performance.
❏ Changes in their personal hygiene or appearance.
❏ Uncharacteristically reckless behaviour.
❏ Bouts of anger.
❏ Diet and weight changes.
❏ Insomnia.
❏ Giving away sentimental or expensive possessions.
❏ Talking about suicide.

Never assume these changes are normal – ask the teenager about these changes, and/or speak to a professional.

Understanding self-harm

❏ It's hard to talk about self-harming behaviours, but very important to do so.
❏ People self-harm for many reasons. Ask why your child is engaging in this behaviour and help them identify healthier, alternative ways to deal with their issue. Dialectical behaviour therapy (DBT) distress tolerance skills are very helpful for this.
❏ Don't dismiss self-harm as just crying out for attention. Seek urgent professional help.

Seek help for yourself

❏ Dealing with the death of a loved one, let alone from a suicide, is incredibly difficult. No one should have to deal with it alone.
❏ Trying to support other family members through grief can be really hard – especially when you need support yourself.

❏ People assume that by going to therapy they're moving on. Therapy is about learning to cope with the loss and having someone to sit with you through your pain so that you're not alone.

Acceptance

❏ Dwelling on the past and what you wish you could have changed or done differently isn't helpful. Focusing on this will leave you stuck and overwhelmed.

❏ Accepting feelings of grief and letting these out can leave you feeling less overwhelmed. Focus on doing something fulfilling to balance the feelings of grief.

Talk about it

❏ Help people to understand how mental illnesses can lead to suicidal behaviour, to shift their stigmatised beliefs, and to realise that suicide is not a sin.

❏ If someone is dealing with grief, don't assume that they will speak to you about their feelings if you don't ask. It's hard to create space to talk about difficult feelings if no one around you asks how you're feeling. If they don't want to talk, they can say so.

❏ Teenagers need someone they trust to talk to. They need ways to let their intense feelings out (dancing, exercising, drawing, etc) and they need guidance about how to manage their feelings effectively.

2

MELISSA DU PREEZ

Depression

Dig a little under the surface of many people with depression and you'll find a family tree mapped by the disorder. For Melissa du Preez, her feelings of despair growing up didn't make sense – after all, there was nothing to be sad about …

My journey with Melissa started ten years ago when, in her early 20s, she was working at the first online news team I was training at a well-known news radio station. What stood out for me immediately was her excellent work ethic and desire to please and do well. This might sound like an obvious require-ment to most people, but sadly this kind of dedication is sorely lacking in most newsrooms today.

We quickly developed a good relationship and worked well together for the next year or so, until I could see that she was becoming disillusioned with her work and appeared 'down' quite a bit. It was difficult, then, to dig too deep to try to find out what was worrying her, although I knew she wanted more out of the job.

After she left, we stayed in touch intermittently, but it would be a few years later that I would get a call from Melissa asking to meet for a chat. It was only then that, knowing of my involvement with SADAG and work on mental health, she started opening up about her own journey.

Interestingly, Melissa had always appeared a confident, competent young woman and, as often happens, I was surprised to hear about her anxiety and depression. At the same time it explained some of the decisions she'd made over the years job-wise, and the questions she'd asked me in between.

Although this story may not be as dramatic as others in this book, I feel it is just as important, as it's a typical story of depression – one to which millions of people will relate. It's also a story of hope that, even though things may seem bleak at times, with the right interventions life's journey can go on shining.

It is a glorious summer's day as we do this interview sitting on my patio, with Melissa's fiancé, Morné, sitting protectively close to her, worried that her retelling her story will upset her. But for Melissa it is important to do this: just maybe, whoever reads it might be able to help someone out there whose depression is undiagnosed.

'In my family, you can't speak to anyone who doesn't have an experience with depression. In fact, some of my aunts and cousins even see the same psychiatrist as me for our meds. For my dad, my depression became apparent when I was quite young and he took the lead in making me talk openly about what I go through and understanding what others struggle with.'

Today, at 34 years old, Melissa feels in control of her life – but there have been bumps along the way, which become apparent as her story unfolds. For many parents in particular, these bumps should stand out as warning signs that all may not be right for your child and that it could be time to intervene.

Melissa's problems started in her first days at school. For

many children, suddenly finding themselves away from familiar and friendly surroundings can be quite daunting. Throw in a few bullies and you have a recipe for disaster than can affect your whole life.

'My panic attacks started back in primary school and even now I still struggle with social anxiety. Bullying became something I had to deal with daily but I'm glad I'm not a kid today with everyone having smartphones. At least for me, when the school day ended, nobody could keep giving me grief. Nowadays, there's never an escape because online trolling infiltrates every corner of our lives. It's terrifying. If there's no time to switch off from the bullying, how do you survive? I'd always feel anxious about the next day's school but at least I had those breaks.'

Bullying today is often the cause of childhood depression and even suicide, which is generally rooted in social media and, as Melissa points out, having a smartphone. And with social pressures meaning that younger and younger kids are getting smartphones, a degree of monitoring might be a good idea.

For some small children, this type of anxiety can lessen as they get older, but this wasn't to be for Melissa.

'As I got older the panic attacks became more severe. My dad would even give me one of his anxiety tablets just so I could fall asleep. It was only when I was 15 that my dad took me to get professional help. He hadn't wanted me to go on to antidepressants when I was a child. He was worried they might alter the state of my brain and change my personality at such a young age. It was also hard for me when I was young to speak to anyone about it. I didn't mind talking to family, though, and I did completely open up to my dad.'

Against what many parents would think, it's been established that antidepressants are safe for children and teens to take. Although there is a warning about an associated risk of increased suicidal thinking and behaviour, the latest research from the Mayo Clinic shows that the benefits of antidepressants may be greater than the risk of suicide (see, for example, https://www.mayoclinic.org/diseases-conditions/teen-depression/in-depth/antidepressants/art-20047502).

Any parent reading this will feel the pain Melissa's parents felt. It's so hard to watch your child suffering and not to be able to do anything to really change things. It's hard for Melissa to talk about her dad, who has now passed away, and I watch her face change when she mentions him. Melissa talks with her eyes and the story she's telling reflects there.

'As you can tell I was extremely close to my dad but my mom was also affected by my being bullied. It seemed as though no one wanted to play with me, which really wasn't fun. I never had many friends at school. I always felt I looked weird with my wild curly hair and I guess I was a depressed, morbid child. I'd always seek out the library as a refuge and volunteered there in my break times. I'd find a quiet corner and read a book.

'I'd do whatever it took to get through the day but there were times, even at primary school, when I thought about suicide but never acted on those thoughts.' I sit there, hearing this. My training as a journalist teaches me not to react but, having a personal relationship with Melissa, this is hard to avoid.

'You really thought about suicide so young?' I ask. Her expression doesn't change as she explains.

'My dad used to keep a gun next to his bed, which I guess he thought was safe in its holster. It was a big, heavy revolver and one day I took it out of the holster trying to figure out how

31

to use it. Luckily the images that popped into my brain at that moment were the stories my father had told me about people's failed attempts at killing themselves and how they were left in a vegetative state, having to rely on someone to look after them for the rest of their lives. No thank you. If taking my life was ever going to be a possibility, I had to choose a way that would definitely end it and not leave anything to chance. I didn't tell my parents about my thoughts – otherwise I don't think I'd ever have been allowed to leave home.'

I'm still a little shocked at this admission and perhaps the fact her dad spoke to her so frankly about this. Did he realise then that this would ever be a possibility for his beloved daughter? As Melissa continues, I can hear the pain in her voice as she vividly recalls some of the worst days of her life.

'School holidays for me didn't mean going away to the coast, but rather a break from the hell that was school. The week before I was due to go back to school the old anxieties would return. I'd talk to myself to prepare for the inevitable, telling myself I was just being silly to worry. It didn't help ...

'Over the years the panic attacks became worse. My stomach would get upset and sleep was difficult. I particularly remember having a panic attack the night before I started my first year of high school. Walking into school that first day with people looking at me, I told myself, "It's just five years."'

If you're imagining an ugly teenager whom no one would want to be with, you'd be wrong. Melissa is and was an attractive, vibrant and energetic young woman, but the mind when you're that age can tell you otherwise, especially when you have depression. Make no mistake – at this already difficult age, depression can weigh heavily on young shoulders without professional help. Perhaps what this story says to parents is to be aware, to stay in touch with your kids' feelings. When they say someone is being horrible to them or they don't want to go to school, look a little further and don't be afraid to seek outside help if you feel you need it. Professional help can change the course of a child's life; Melissa just battled on.

'High school meant one thing – new place, new bullies,' Melissa goes on. 'People are cruel and I often wonder whether behaving so terribly makes them feel better about themselves – I really don't know. When I think I've been mean to someone or made them feel bad, then I feel really bad. I hate to hurt someone's feelings.'

This I know to be true. When I worked with Melissa in the newsroom there would be times when I'd be giving the team, including Melissa, hell for sloppy work. It would take weeks before she would very reluctantly tell me the source of the problem – one of her colleagues whom she didn't want to get into trouble. She would rather take the pain than stir up problems for anyone else.

'One particularly traumatic and triggering event for my dad was during a family dinner at a local mall. We were sitting at a table in a restaurant when some boys from my school walked past, looked our way and started laughing. That was all I needed to go into a full-on panic attack that brought the dinner to a halt. As we were leaving I was crying and hyperventilating. My brother was telling me to just calm down while my father was swearing – I'd never seen him so helpless. He kept talking to himself, asking "What do I do?", not expecting an answer. He didn't know how to help me right then but this was the motivator to get some serious help.'

Melissa pauses, as if recalling it takes her breath away again. This was the turning point for Melissa's family, which saw them realising that professional medical help was needed. For many families the thought of putting your child on medication is daunting but, when weighed up against the alternatives, there is no option. More and more children, perhaps under today's heavy pressures, need this kind of help and teachers need to learn to spot these signs as early as possible.

'This finally led to me seeing our family doctor who put me on an antidepressant, which I stayed on for the next ten years. At first I remember feeling numb – not really feeling anything. The manic highs and lows somehow level off. You don't miss the lows but you do miss the highs.' I can hear the honesty in the way she makes this admission.

'I think even more than the actual effect of the medication I felt better knowing I wasn't just imagining what was happening to me and that finally I was doing something to gain control. It was a definite line in the sand and I knew if I stepped over it what would happen. Although this didn't change the bullying, now I could see a little clearer through the fog of my life.'

Simply being told by a mental health professional that you're not just a moody kid can make a big difference in a child's life. Melissa was also particularly lucky to have a dad she could turn to. For many teenagers this isn't something they feel they can do, fearing that 'no one understands what I'm going through'. It is vital for your child to know you're there for them, to listen, help and guide them, particularly in situations such as this.

'Having a dad so open to listening to me helped me identify when an episode was coming and I could reach out to him. When this happens it feels like beetles scratching their way up from the base of my skull, tightening my neck. Today, especially with my partner Morné by my side, I can take it in my stride.

34

'Funnily enough, I loved schoolwork and thrived at exam time because I could focus on problems and swotting. Lessons were also good because all I had to do was pay attention to the teacher. Whatever was going on in the rest of my life, such as my parents fighting at home, nothing else mattered right then.'

Something Melissa has never mentioned to me before was what happened to her mom. I'd always heard about her dad, and had seen the many photos she shared on Facebook of their times together. I wondered whether this part of the interview would be hard for her but I could see she'd long ago come to terms with this episode of her life.

'My mom left one night when I was in Grade 10, or Standard 8 as it was called then. I was 16 and my older brother was writing his matric prelim exams. She was very involved in boy scouts and had gone out, saying she had a planning meeting for the following year. There was no word from her until two days later when she called my gran to say she was in Zimbabwe with another man. Just a few weeks later, my parents were divorced.

'Funnily enough it didn't hit me that badly then. I'd always been closer to my dad and all my focus right then was on helping my brother through his prelims. The feelings of abandonment only came later.' Only a brief look of anguish passes over her face at this remark.

Melissa had always dreamed of being a writer. When her dad suggested journalism as a good stepping stone, she enrolled in what was then considered one of the best courses in the country, at Pretoria Technikon, as it was known. I hear the enthusiasm in her voice and see the light come back into her eyes.

'This whole experience was so much better than school for me. I loved the course and did really well. I had wonderful opportunities to do internship work and spent some time working at a well-known Pretoria-based radio station.

'All the way through my degree and internships, I was coping well with my emotions. One day, on my way to work, I had a car accident. A man, who I thought I recognised, arrived at the scene and offered to help me. It turned out he was the head of a rival radio station. After calling my dad to tell him what had happened, he then offered to drive me to my office. He asked if I was interested in being involved in news, which was the main thrust of his station. Before I knew it, I'd had an interview and was offered a job as a writer and subeditor on their first online news team.

'Although it was exciting to be working in such a busy newsroom, what I really wanted was to be out reporting stories, but because I was really good at subediting I was more use to them behind a desk. They did, however, offer me reporting work over weekends, which I grabbed, determined to show them I could be an asset out there. I also made some great friends at the station, who I'm still really close to.'

What Melissa hadn't factored into her plan was the toll that subediting in the week and reporting on weekends would take on her. A year later, she found herself completely burnt out. At the time, I could see a change in her and sensed something was wrong, but I didn't know the full extent of the problem. She was an expert at hiding her real emotions. Added to all this, boyfriend problems pushed things even closer to the brink.

While we're growing up, no one teaches us about working with our emotions. Rather, we learn how to block and avoid them – the worst thing you can do for good mental or physical health.

'At this time the station where I'd been an intern made me an offer to return there full-time, which I took. I was coping really well until I met a guy – a totally unsuitable guy – and started what turned out to be a disastrous relationship. Once again the work proved too stressful and I moved to an NGO, also in Pretoria, where I was now living with my boyfriend. Eventually I realised this guy was never going to change and I didn't want to share his life with drink and drugs. It was only after my dad said, "I love him but I love you more," that we broke up. Like all breakups it's never easy, particularly when you have depression lurking in the background.

'When I met Morné, my fiancé, he knew about my depression and that I was on antidepressants. That's the first thing I get out in the open when I start a new relationship. I don't care whether the person believes in the medication or not. I know what's wrong with me and how to deal with it. I tell them it's not a big deal. I'll tell you when it's happening but you must just carry on with your life. I explain there will be times when it's going to be hard and you're not going to know how to deal with me. You're going to think that it has something to do with you, but it's nothing you've done …'

Morné's arm goes out to rest on her shoulder and I see the immediate comforting effect this has. He constantly glances at her during the interview, as if he wants to whisk her away if the emotions become too strong.

Melissa goes quiet for a moment. As she leans forward, her long, thick hair partly covers her face, and her voice is thick with emotion as she starts to talk about her father's death.

'In 2016, I lost my dad after a short illness. This sparked the worst episode I've ever gone through. The following year I had a really bad breakdown when I realised that I didn't know how to exist without him. It's like starting your life from scratch. Even today I'll sometimes start crying because I miss him so much. He was the centre of my world and I guess I'm still figuring out how to cope with his loss.' She pauses, closes her eyes, takes a deep breath and brushes away the tears.

'He'd remarried a wonderful woman a couple of years after his divorce and she still plays an important role in my life. And of course I have my aunts, cousins and friends who are always there for me. I do worry sometimes what would happen if one of them suddenly leaves – what would I do?'

One of the most common threads that run through stories about mental health is support, or lack of it. Just being there for someone – not judging, just being there and listening – can help greatly. Seeing a mental health professional helps even more.

'When I felt the grief catching up with me I went to see a psychologist, which always helps. I also explained to my boss about my depression and asked for time off to go and see someone as my work was suffering. I think they understood this was serious and agreed to give me time to work through it.

'I went to a psychiatrist who changed my medication and this really helped, as I'm still on the same prescription today.

'I met Morné, who worked with my brother, a few years ago. I think I was a bit of a pest at first, calling him on my way home from work to suggest meeting for coffee.' Morné nods in agreement and laughs, throwing his head back and blushing a little behind his bushy beard.

'He'd try and get rid of me but I wasn't going to give up. I could tell he was a loner and pretty much self-isolating. My goal became getting him to talk.' Melissa is animated. 'At the start of our relationship we'd just meet for coffee. We'd talk about people we worked with, and I'd maybe suggest the per-son he was having problems with was possibly dealing with something in their life, so maybe to approach things from a different angle. Now the way he tackles things is a lot different. We've helped each other so much.'

When they'd first met, Melissa had brought Morné to meet me. I could immediately see just how comfortable they were with each other and how much Morné cared for her. This was just what Melissa needed then – someone she could be herself with, all the ups and downs included.

I ask Morné to tell me how Melissa has impacted his life. He is naturally shy but comes alive when talking about the two things that mean the most to him – technology and Melissa.

'Before I met Melissa I don't think I'd ever met anyone else with depression and I struggled to understand what she was going through. Back then I thought that when someone said they were depressed they would "get over it" with time. At the beginning of our friendship I have to say it wasn't easy going. It could be overwhelming to talk to her sometimes and I'd have to distance myself to avoid a spiral.

'She was completely open about her depression and at the beginning I had to learn quickly how to juggle it all. I'd lost my parents when I was young – my mom in high school and my dad when I was 21 – so I'm no stranger to depression but for me it was driven by a situation, whereas Melissa will sometimes fall into a spiral from stress or anxiety. I was used to working out my problems on my own but then Melissa came along and we became inseparable.'

'Over the years this friendship has grown into a strong part-nership and engagement,' says Melissa, glancing down at her ring. 'Whatever's happening to me in terms of dealing with my depression, although he's never understood what it's like, he's always been open to listening and learning.' Morné nods, and squeezes her hand.

39

But there's one dark area of her life that won't change. 'From now on there will never be an event or milestone in my life that my dad will be a part of. There's no one to walk me down the aisle, to feel proud when I get a promotion or even buy a house – that's a lonely feeling.

'There are a few things that help bring me out of a slump. One is to keep busy and not let my mind dwell for too long. For me that could mean sewing, writing or spending time around other people. I have to wear myself out before my head hits the pillow.'

'Melissa helped guide me by sharing information from groups like the South African Depression and Anxiety Group and countless articles online,' explains Morné. 'I've read about the chemical side and how the brain reacts to the lack of serotonin. But none of this explained how a partner can help or respond. They all say the same thing: be there for the person. What does that really mean? I take things very literally. I follow instructions. Nothing really tells you that if you have a partner with depression these are the things you need to look out for. These are the signs that say what they're going through. After four years together, I start picking up on signs that something's coming and pre-empt it by keeping her busy and distracted.

'When I see her going into a deep slump, talking about how pointless everything seems, I try to be supportive and not undervalue her thoughts at the time. That's the thing, she knows that her thoughts can become scattered and illogical but she can't control them and that's when it's up to me to be her voice of reason.

'I've recently gone through a situation in my personal life that prompted me to reach out to a psychologist myself. Before

I met Melissa, I wouldn't have done this and probably thought it was a sign of weakness but I know better now.

'Even though I'd read so much about depression, when it happened to me I didn't see it coming. It doesn't happen overnight – it slowly creeps up. It's changed our relationship as now I understand Melissa more. She's made me look at people and things differently. I look at alternative ways of doing things and consider what other people may be dealing with themselves before I turn to judgement, and that's something I wouldn't change for the world.'

A theme that runs throughout the stories in this book is the need for structure: having something to do, somewhere to go, and not to have to stay still and just think, letting your thoughts run away with you. This is where Melissa has come a long way.

'I deal differently with crises these days also. Instead of dealing with my feelings about the problem, I first deal with the issue and then how I feel later. If someone says to me they're not sure if they should see a therapist or talk to someone, I say *yes* – go talk to them. Sometimes it means trying a few different therapists before finding one who suits you. It's the same with medications. You may have to try a few before finding what works for you.'

As our interview comes to a close, Melissa looks sheepish as she tells me, 'I still talk to myself – honestly. This is just about being true to yourself and not disclosing to everyone around you. It would probably overwhelm them. If you're sitting in bed in the dark of night, at the loneliest time you can just spiral. But these days, even though occasionally I feel terrible, I don't feel like reaching for a gun as I know it will pass. These days I can see the way out.'

TOOLBOX TIPS

Managing panic in children

❏ Understand panic attacks and how to manage them, so *you* don't panic when they happen. There are simple ways to manage them. Here are some helpful links: https://www.psycom.net/ help-kids-with-anxiety; https://www.psycom.net/kids-coping-skills-anxiety; https://blogs.psychcentral.com/ anxious-kids/2016/09/what-to-do-when-your-child-is-suffering-from-panic-attacks/

❏ Mindfulness is a great way to manage anxiety. There are many apps to help – Headspace, Smiling Mind, Calm and Insight Timer are a few.

Sticks and stones can break your bones but words can never harm you: not true!

❏ Bullying can significantly affect a child's mental health, with long-term repercussions. If your child is being bullied, seek professional assistance.

❏ Many children don't speak about bullying because they fear their parents' reactions. Be sure to listen first. Find ways to deal with the issue that your child feels comfortable with, instead of going over their heads and dealing with it on your own.

❏ Here's a link to a very helpful website: https://www. stopbullying.gov/

They're just kids, it's not such a big deal

❏ Children also experience depression and suicidality – it's not something to be dismissed. If your child is struggling, ask them what they're thinking – talking about suicide doesn't increase the risk, it opens up space to talk and get the help they need.

❏ A gun dramatically increases risk of suicide. Children are impulsive; it's easier to act on impulse if they have access to harmful objects.

Parents also need support

❏ Many parents feel helpless when their child is in pain. It's hard to accept your limitations when it comes to protecting your children, so it's important to have your own space to process this.

❏ You're not expected to have all the answers or always take the pain away. Remember, just being there to listen and support them can make all the difference.

Depression comes and goes: learn to recognise the warning signs

❏ Depression is episodic, so even if you've felt fine for a long time, it's not uncommon to find yourself depressed again when going through a difficult time.

❏ It's not a weakness to ask for help, but a great strength. Learn to recognise events that trigger your depression, so you can mobilise your support network before sinking into depression.

Take a break

❏ It's hard to speak about mental health with others, but is necessary if you're not coping.

❏ Everyone needs a break from time to time, but won't necessarily be given one without asking for it.

3

DARYL BROWN

A suicide attempt

I first met Daryl Brown in 2016 when he was a guest speaker at a SADAG media workshop on reporting responsibly on mental health that I was facilitating in Cape Town. I'd spoken to him on the phone about the workshop and had been struck by his warm, friendly nature and his positive outlook on life – this from a man who, three years previously, had tried to take his own life. I was looking forward to meeting him.

It was only when I saw this good-looking young man with a huge smile wheeling himself into the room that I realised it: not only had he attempted suicide, but in the process he'd lost his legs. How could someone have gone through that and still radiate such a love of life?

Daryl has this effect on everyone he meets and is a wonderful example of the power of the human spirit. But getting to where he is today hasn't been easy.

It is 2019 when I meet Daryl again to do this interview at a coffee shop in Cape Town's Waterfront. He manoeuvres his way through tables with agility so that we can sit outside overlooking the harbour while we chat. It has been about 18 months since I've seen him at another media workshop, and I can see that in this short time his confidence and sense of who he is has developed even further. Now, sitting across a table from him, drinking coffee, I'm eager to find out more about what led him to that tragic 2016 day.

We go back to his early years, growing up in sleepy Melkbosstrand on the southwestern coast of the Cape. This sounds like the perfect childhood, but it wasn't for everyone. If you didn't fit into the mould of small-town society, life could be tricky.

'Arriving halfway through Grade 1 in Melkbosstrand from the Eastern Cape meant everyone had already formed their groups of friends, so I started my school life feeling like a bit of an outsider. I didn't know it then, but that would lay the foundation for most of my school life.

'Even the one best friend I made in Grade 4 emigrated to New Zealand and I never seemed to connect with anyone after that. By the time I was in Grade 6 at the age of around 11, the bullying suddenly had the word "gay" attached to it. I had no idea, then, what that even was, and I don't think they did either, but it was their way of telling me I was girlish – and they were right. At first I quite enjoyed the attention. Then the penny dropped and I realised this wasn't seen as a good thing.

'I'd always got along better with girls but little girls don't always want to play with boys – even feminine ones. From an early age, when I played make-believe games I'd always play the female character and was also romantically more attracted to boys than girls, but of course it was very vague when I was small.

'By Grade 7, without a single close friend to confide in, I felt very alone and that I'd almost rather not be around. My parents were dealing with marital and business problems then and I really didn't know how to talk to them about things or to

45

articulate what I was feeling. This was when my first thoughts of suicide started. I figured it would be much easier for everyone if I wasn't around and I wouldn't have to figure out all this emotional and sexual stuff. The thought of moving on to high school terrified me even more, especially as we didn't even have a high school in Melkbosstrand, meaning a daily commute to Table View on a school bus – bullying on wheels.'

What many people don't realise is that there is no age limit for depression. The youngest recorded suicide that SADAG is aware of is that of a six-year-old child from Ekurhuleni. Daryl's childhood feelings are not uncommon. If anything, with social media today bullying can be even worse. Children are often reluctant to get their parents involved in 'stuff' that's going down at school, feeling it could make things even worse. But parents must find a way to keep tabs on their children's mental health: Daryl's story could be your story.

Initially, Daryl remained ever the optimist. 'Even though I'd had thoughts of ending it all, somewhere in the back of my mind when things were really bad was the thought that if something would change, life could be better. So perhaps high school in a whole new area wouldn't be that bad and maybe I'd make some friends who wouldn't notice my being differ-ent. But of course nothing changed and high school was just a continuation of primary school hell.

'At home, with no friends to hang out with or have sleepovers with, I'd stay in my room reading, which was my escape. Even though my solitude worried her, this was a way my mom and I connected as she's a librarian. With her own pressing problems right then she just didn't have time or energy left over to worry about me too much – but she knew something wasn't right.

'I knew I was sad a lot but I didn't know the word

"depression" then at all. I might have heard it – but I had no idea what it meant or the concept. I certainly didn't know what a psychiatrist or psychologist did.'

According to his mom Roelda, she knew he had problems in his last year at primary school. 'I felt the teachers did nothing about them and by the time he went to high school I think he just became good at hiding his real feelings. All through university and his first job he was constantly busy, with hobbies and the church, while completing two degrees seamlessly. It's always been his way of coping with life, I think. Staying really busy. Sometimes I'd wonder if he wasn't exhausting himself. But my thoughts were always balanced with the fact that, unlike many other children, he never experimented with drugs, drank or smoked. He was a good boy,' she explains.

Daryl was acutely aware of his standing in the family. 'I have a brother who is four years younger and the polar opposite of me. He's always been very sporty and, when he was young, quite a troublemaker at school, whereas I excelled academically and was always well behaved, meaning my parents' focus was generally on him, not me. I was the good child. They'd say, we don't have to worry about Daryl – he's managing. Little did they know. I only found out years later that my brother got into a fight with another kid at primary school because this guy called me a fag.'

Daryl did find a group of friends at high school, but with none of them living close to him, hanging out after school was difficult. 'I still felt like an outsider and so I kept myself apart from everyone. I felt like I had to hide my true self – being gay and feminine. I even got good at dropping my voice.

'By high school, though, I knew the word "gay". At the same time I railed against it because I was quite religious and knew

47

this was sinful and wrong. I'd pray for God to heal me. I also prayed that when I woke up I'd be a girl, which would make my life so much easier. I didn't have serious body dysmorphia or feel unhappy with my body but thought if I was a girl my feelings towards guys would make sense and I could legitimately get the attention I wanted. It also had to be easier to be a girl because they could be open about their feelings.

'I never discussed any of these thoughts with my parents, and living in Melkbosstrand there was no one else I knew like me. My dad had two gay cousins in Cape Town and one took me under his wing and started taking me to the theatre – but he never mentioned homosexuality or being gay. I think he felt awkward as he didn't have kids of his own and wasn't sure where boundaries were drawn. I did connect with him but we never had a real discussion, which again added to my isolation.

'As each year passed I would have this hope that next year would be better. When I left high school things would be better, I told myself. I'm innately an optimist, which is probably why I lasted so long before my suicide attempt.'

Sadly, although LGBTQI+ rights and acceptance have come a long way, homophobia is alive and well in our communities today. Children's opinions and understanding of homosexuality generally come from their parents. If parents realised the damage that their casual, often biased comments could cause, maybe they'd think twice about the opinions they're forming in their children's minds.

'My big hopes were pinned on a new life when I went to university to study marketing communication. I didn't really hide that I was gay, but at the same time I found it hard to accept that part of myself. This made it easy to bully or mock me because they knew it would actually matter to me, whereas

48

someone openly gay would have shrugged it off.

'And then, once again, when I started working I told myself my life had to change and to a degree it did. When I finally decided to come out I was also becoming more religious – not a great mix. I'd been taught that feelings of lust and "unnatural" feelings were sinful, and by matric I'd started going to a different church than my parents' Methodist one, a far more evangelical one.

'I became very involved there, joining the young adult leadership and helping with the kids' holiday club. This was also when my praying intensified, beseeching God to heal me. I'd do whatever it took, including periods of fasting – but of course nothing changed. One of the guys at work said that I reminded him of a character in the television programme *Glee* because he was a gay character, and I could see the resemblance but it still made me uncomfortable.'

Looking for help in all the wrong places is a well-known saying, and is just what Daryl did. Turning to religion is a common theme for people with mental health issues. They feel so alone in their world, desperately wanting help but not knowing where to turn. Psychologists or psychiatrists would mean they're crazy – but religion is acceptable, and easy to cling to. For many this can be a good thing, as a spiritual advisor can sometimes act as a therapist. But for Daryl this certainly wasn't the case.

'By then I'd also come out to our young pastor. I confided in him that nothing was changing for me and I needed help to overcome the spiritual conflict I found myself in. He was a very sweet, typical Afrikaans rugby oke, just a few years older than me. He told me he really wanted to help me but had no idea how. I told him I'd read a book by the director of an organisation called Exodus International. They called themselves an "ex-gay ministry" and held workshops and camps worldwide where people could go to become straight! The director professed to be "ex-gay" himself, with a wife and children. I was so inspired by his story I wrote to him asking if they had an office in Cape Town. They responded by saying they don't have an office but do have someone who was affiliated with them who ran a support group for people who were gay and wanted help to change. I got this guy's details and asked my pastor if he'd come with me to meet him in case he was a weirdo.

'My pastor was impressed because it was immediately apparent that this guy knew his scripture quite well so it was agreed he'd mentor me. I was 22 at the time and he was 30. I started opening up to him and for the first time I could talk openly about how I felt, as he'd been through this himself. It was also the first time someone gave me affirmation of myself. He was very supportive and also quite attractive and so I developed a bit of a crush on him. Then, about three months after he'd started mentoring me, I lost my virginity to him. This to the ex-gay man!

'Suddenly, after always being there for me he didn't respond to any of my messages. This went on for around a week. I couldn't understand what had happened because we'd started declaring our love for each other and he even offered me a job as his assistant. A week later I heard from him that we can't be open about our relationship but we could keep helping each other out this way ... I couldn't deal with that. I didn't want to feel that I was doing something wrong all the time and have to sneak around.

'The reason I had come out to my pastor was that I wanted to find answers as to why God made me this way. Was it wrong? I wanted to investigate this without feeling I had to hide or that someone from church was going to see me. I wanted to be open about my life and now this man was telling me we could see each other – but no one must know. I stopped seeing him and decided to take up a former boss's invitation to visit her in London for a couple of weeks.'

Sadly, mental illness doesn't just go away with a change of scenery – it will follow you wherever you go. Without intervention it's there to stay.

'By the time I returned home things had happened at the church and everything seemed to be in chaos. So for some reason I decided this was a good time to come out to my parents and the world. My parents weren't really surprised, although I still don't really know what they felt. Feelings weren't something we spoke about in our family – at least not until after my suicide attempt. My dad said, "You're still my son and I still love you." It felt like he was reading from a script and I didn't really know how he felt.

'I came out by sending an email to my parents, my church friends and all my colleagues on the same day. I needed to do it in one go. My colleagues still teased me that this happened after spending two weeks in my boss's pink bedroom in London, where pink was everywhere – even the computer was pink. I thought once I'd come out I'd feel fine – perfect, even – but it didn't change what I felt inside. *So now what?* I thought. I discovered that changing external things doesn't change depression.

'At this point I'd been living with depression for 11 years. I'd always thought the word "depression" meant you were mad or crazy, or it was a word bored housewives made up so they

51

could talk about their problems.

'When I thought of speaking to a therapist or talking to my parents I knew neither would be able to say something that would magically make everything better. I didn't understand then how therapy would be able to help me and didn't want to burden my parents. I thought my parents, family and friends all have their own problems which they seem to deal with – why can't I deal with mine? I would suck it up and carry on.'

'Only as my boys grew up did I notice they were very different,' explains Roelda. 'I suspected Daryl was gay and when he was in high school I brought it up, saying this was fine with me. He assured me he wasn't and that he liked girls. In those days in particular he was very involved in the church and loved the structure around it, the singing, holiday activities and the community. So when he did come out and the church didn't handle it so well, this was tough for him. He even said because he was a Christian he was going to remain celibate, which my husband, his brother and I all said he didn't have to do. We said this wasn't normal or even healthy and told him to just be himself. But this was hard for him.'

About a year later, Daryl decided to escape to London and do his master's degree. 'By then I was disillusioned with marketing, particularly when it came to deadline time with everyone freaking out and dealing with the work pressure. I'd think, *Why are we doing this to ourselves? We're not really helping anyone or making the world a better place.* I simply couldn't find any meaning in my work.

'I enrolled in a private university in the City of London and found accommodation with some other students not far from campus. London, right from my first visit, gave me a sense of freedom I didn't feel in South Africa. I'd always hidden my homosexuality, avoiding certain music because it was too gay, or dressing too flamboyantly. I'd been doing this for so long it took me years to unpack this and embrace who I was. But in London somehow I could breathe and just be myself, so when I moved there I assumed that magically everything would be fine and I could be the true me.'

With depression, it doesn't matter where you are or what's happening to you. You could be on a yacht cruising around the world or living the life of your dreams, but without help it doesn't just go away. Daryl's dream seemed to come true when he met what he thought was the ideal partner.

'The magic started happening, I thought, when I started my first open romantic relationship with a lovely guy I met there. I still had a lot of issues that I needed to work through and he struggled with that. Although he was quite out there and camp, his family were more anti-gay than mine. I knew we weren't really compatible but I didn't want to let go of the relationship. I told myself this was it and I would never meet anyone else. The inevitable breakup was the worst I'd ever had. I was devastated, and at the same time after finishing my studies I was battling to find a job that would sponsor me to stay in London.

'I thought, *I'm going to have to go back to Cape Town with my tail between my legs, live with my parents and leech off them forever*. One problem and issue after another was compounding my misery – and my depression. Added to which I didn't get the results I'd hoped for with my master's because of all the distractions. I felt like a complete failure and for the first time couldn't think of a single other thing I could do to fix my depression. I tried everything and was exhausted from trying and waiting for this one day when everything would feel okay. Obviously, this day would never come. I couldn't keep on waiting – I couldn't do it. I thought my parents would be better off not having to support me and my friends would be better off not hearing me complain. Not that I really did that, because I was always scared of becoming that person – a moaner. This was partly why my relationship didn't work: because I wouldn't open up to my partner and be honest about what I was feeling and what I wanted, as I thought the more he knew about me the less he'd like me. I just wanted to go to sleep and never wake up.'

When someone decides to take their own life, their plans are generally well thought out and they become expert manipulators. Daryl convinced his friends in London that he was going back to South Africa and shut down his Facebook account so they wouldn't know he hadn't left.

'Looking back, if someone had really sat me down and asked what was going on I may have opened up and starting talking about my thoughts. I was waiting for my ex-boyfriend to say something that would give me hope, a sign – but nothing. Although I'm not sure what anyone could have said that would have changed my mind.

'I gave my landlord a month's notice and on the day I was supposed to leave I packed a suitcase, went down to the nearest tube station and waited for the platform to empty. It was a Sunday afternoon so I knew it would be relatively quiet. I waited for the next train and jumped onto the tracks in front of it.

'Before I did this there was nothing going through my mind. No second thoughts. Once I'd made this decision and given notice, it felt as though this huge weight had been lifted off my shoulders because I knew that I just had to hang around for one more month and it would all be over. I was even playing a game of Sudoku on my phone while I sat on the platform waiting for the train.

'I didn't want to create any chance of anyone finding out what I'd planned and so, although I sent my mom an email, I made sure this was to her work address and she wouldn't get it until the next day – too late to do anything about it. When she did see it, she and my dad were frantically trying to find me. They didn't have any other contact numbers for me in London or anyone else who knew me. I'd written a note and had put it in a bag on the platform, giving details of my next of kin, but somehow these were never found. Eventually they found me through Interpol and I still feel bad about what I put them through for those three days of uncertainty.'

This highlights the difference between Daryl's thinking before his suicide attempt, without any intervention, and afterwards, on medication: he first just wanted to do whatever it would take to end his life, which moved to thinking about what he had put his family through.

As Daryl's story unfolds, I see him feeling the mental anguish he'd gone through at that time. It's hard recalling these events, but Daryl knows how important it is and he pauses occasionally to take deep breaths before continuing with his story.

'The next thing I remember after jumping was lying underneath the train. It was just black and somehow felt too mundane to be the afterlife. So I just lay there and my first thought was, *Fuck – it didn't happen*. I slowly regained sensation and I could feel that my legs had been ripped off but there wasn't that much pain yet. I couldn't move my arms or my head and I was suddenly terrified I was paralysed. I think it was just the shock that froze me. Eventually the pain became excruciating. I could hear people getting off the train above me and remember thinking there's going to be all these parents with little kids who they're taking to the museum and little old ladies, so I can't scream or yell now because I'll just traumatise them. I remember the rescue team crawling towards me from the front of the train but it felt like they were taking forever. Eventually I shouted that they must please come quicker – it hurts. There was suddenly a massive silence. It was at this point that they realised I was alive and I could now hear them moving faster.

'The first guy reached me and introduced himself – though I can't remember his name. He said, "We're going to help you," and I said, "My legs are gone – right?" He looked down and said to one of his team members, "This is a mess." The whole time I was trying to pass out. I thought if I lose consciousness there's still a chance I won't make it. There's still a chance it could work. But the paramedic was urging me to open my eyes and stay conscious. I didn't and the next memory was waking up in the Royal London Hospital where I'd been airlifted. I found out later that the rescue team had tried to reattach one of my legs on the platform but by the time we reached the hospital it was infected so had to be removed.

'I wasn't responding to the medical team in hospital – I was just thinking, *Please, let me go.* I ignored all their questions. Then two nurses started wheeling me somewhere and I was fading in and out of consciousness. I remember being in a lift when one of the nurses asked, "Where are we taking him?" and the other said, "We're taking him for a scan because he's not responding to anything." That's when I opened my eyes and the male nurse introduced himself as Chris and held my hand. He told me they thought I wasn't with them and I told him I was pretending because I'd really wanted this to work. I lost consciousness shortly after this but know that he never let go of my hand that whole time.

'He came to visit me in the trauma ward several weeks later and asked if I remembered what I said to him when I woke up – that I didn't want to be alive. I said yes and he asked, how did I feel now? I told him that I still kind of wished I wasn't alive. I wasn't okay before and now I'm the same, minus legs. I feel bad about saying that to him because he was a really good nurse and so kind to me. I felt like I was taking some meaning of his job away from him.'

You probably breathed out when you read the part about Daryl still being alive – and maybe then read on with amazement that instead of feeling relieved that he wasn't dead, he was disappointed. This is common with people who attempt suicide. They don't do this lightly – they don't want to live any longer and not getting it right is often the biggest disappointment of their lives.

'During this time there was a team of psychiatrists in the hospital who put me on antidepressants, but I didn't see a psychologist then. As I didn't have anyone to go home to, they kept me in the trauma ward for about eight weeks. During this time I saw a lot of patients come and go. Every two or three days the psychiatrists would check in on me to check my vitals and my suicidal ideation and mental health. They had a checklist – was I sleeping? Was I eating?'

We generally think that people who survive a suicide attempt won't try again, but just the opposite is true. Within the first three months to a year following a suicide attempt, people are at the highest risk of a second attempt – and of maybe succeeding.

When Roelda Brown arrived at work on the Monday and

saw Daryl's email in her inbox, she opened it without worrying about the contents. 'After all, the day before we were sending WhatsApps about the latest JK Rowling book I'd read. But as soon as I read the first few lines of his email I knew something beyond terrible had happened and the thoughts that went through my mind were, *He's either jumped in front of a train or into a river*. I prayed it was a train as if it was a river I thought I'd never know what happened to him.

'On the Sunday evening, after our WhatsApp book chat, I wanted to send him another message telling him how much I missed him and that he should come home. And then I thought no, that's really clingy and I didn't want to be one of those mothers hanging on to her son. I realised, after, that the same time I was thinking this was the moment he jumped.

'After reading the email I immediately told my boss I had to go home; my brain went into some sort of auto mode. We went straight to the police to try and help us find him. Once we discovered what he'd done I was scared because I knew if he survived, the consequences would be serious. His letter had been so full of pain that I actually hoped for his sake he was dead. People, when they hear that, can't understand – and think this makes me a terrible mother – but I could feel the heartbreak and agony in every word of that letter.

'It took a few days to track him down and I was still numb with shock. I remember going into his bedroom and looking at the photos of him and his friends looking so happy, and thinking, *What's the point of all this*? My husband and younger son were angry and kept on saying, "Why didn't he just come home?"

'I'd been a bit worried about him during July and had written to him several times because I knew he was having money problems. I said I couldn't finance him in England but summer was coming and he'd soon be finished with his degree, so he should come home and we'd take it from there. I later realised by then my words were too late.

'One of his best friends had spent two weeks with him in August and I'd asked her to let me know if she thought something was wrong. She had a great time as he showed her all over London and she assured me he was fine. When I saw him in London in hospital I asked him if he'd already made his suicide plans when she was there and he replied, "Yes, I couldn't wait for her to go so I could kill myself." She didn't notice anything and when I told her what had happened over the phone she couldn't believe it either. People who attempt suicide are very good at hiding their true feelings and thoughts.'

'Two weeks later, after waiting for her visa, my mom came to see me,' Daryl continues. 'She stayed with a pastor friend of someone in her church and came to visit me every single day and sat with me as long as she could. But instead of being relieved to see her, I took out all my rage, disappointment and bitterness on her. I was awful to her but she never snapped back at me once. She never got angry. She sat there and took it all.' As Daryl tells me about his mom, for the first time in our interview tears form in his eyes and the emotion momentarily overcomes him.

Could we have stopped him? This is the big question that every family member and friend of someone who has taken their own life asks, as did Roelda. 'Now I think I'm past that but in the beginning you feel worthless,' she explains. 'You must have done something terrible to someone, to the world. I didn't know what, but it must have been bad for something like this to happen.

'Being a librarian, I read many books and first-hand accounts of similar stories and it hit me that those people weren't all bad. If something like that could happen to them, why couldn't it happen to me also?

'When I got to England I said to Daryl, "I can't fix this." When he started coming out of the effect of the morphine he said, "Yes, I know what you mean – you can't fix this." So we just had to go on from there and it wasn't easy. He was angry. Very angry. He felt he'd made a mess of things, not even being able to kill himself successfully. It's hard for a mother to hear this.'

Daryl continues, 'I had a few surgeries and then they eventually moved me to a rehab centre where for the first time I saw a psychologist, Louise. She was blind and I don't know if it was because of this or that she was just a really good psychologist but from the first five minutes of meeting me she saw right through me.

'When I'd tell her stories about things that had happened to me, the things people said to me, I'd try and protect the people in the stories because I didn't want her to form a negative view or judge them on the open interaction we had. But it was as though she'd been in those interactions with me, so she understood exactly how I felt and thought. For the first time I thought, *I'm not crazy and I'm not alone. There's someone who understands how I feel.* She was trained to do this and knew how to get me through this and help me out of it. That was the first time I felt hope again. I could get out of this.'

As we move on to the healing part of his story, his demeanour changes and I see the Daryl I first met – energy and passion return to his voice. 'Another person who helped not just my body but my mind was my amazing physiotherapist. I'd spend six hours a day, every day, with her. She was only a few years older than me and everyone else there was over 50. People who'd had strokes or had limbs amputated due to diabetes as well as those learning to walk with prostheses. She had to work out other exercises for me to, do such as getting into a wheelchair from the floor. It was hard not to form a really close relationship with her during this time, and we're still friends today.

'One day, a woman arrived who'd played volleyball in the Paralympics. She also wasn't using prostheses and they'd asked her to spend an hour with me. She told me she'd lost her legs in one of the London tube bombings and spoke to me about the adjustments she'd made in her life. We laughed over how she'd broken her friend's toilet seat while pulling on her pants. I totally understood as this was a complex manoeuvre. It was good to see the light side and have positive reinforcement.

'While I'd been in the trauma ward for those eight weeks I just felt angry, hurt and disappointed. I questioned my relationship with God and didn't know how I felt. I needed someone to direct my anger at – and it was Him. It was only when I started my rehab and built that relationship with the physio and psychologist that I regained some hope. Spending all that time in the gym and doing something physical really helped, and I was becoming independent again as I'd been worried I'd have to rely on other people. In fact, I felt stronger and fitter than I'd ever been in my life. I felt good. I could do this. It was almost as though the physical disability gave me something to overcome. It motivated me and gave me a purpose and I regained some of that old optimism.'

By this time Daryl's medications had kicked in and his therapy, together with the physical healing, was starting to work.

Daryl was 26 when he returned to South Africa in 2013 and was hit by the realisation of just how isolated he'd been in London. 'Before I left home I'd always felt on the outskirts of my friendship circles and thought no one would notice if I wasn't around. When I came back I discovered that a friend had gone around to all my friends, even ones she didn't know, and got messages from all of them, which he put into a book for me. Some were anecdotes of things I'd done for people or times we'd spent together. Others were just messages of what I meant to people and for the first time I realised that people loved me and I was making a difference in people's lives. If felt amazing and has made me work a lot harder at my friendships. Now I understand how much they actually matter.

'It also made my family and friends more aware of how important it is to tell each other how much we love each other. You assume your family in particular know you love them but hearing it and saying it makes such a difference. It's so important.

'There have been times since I've been back when my thoughts have turned to leaving the country again but then I realise how much I'd miss the people who've known me forever.'

According to Roelda, 'Daryl's come a long way today and he says he's happier now in spite of his disability. This is something people don't understand about him. They focus on his disability and don't hear when I say to them that his disability isn't the worst part of him. Disability, especially when you're young, can be overcome, but depression is something completely different.'

'Another realisation,' Daryl says, 'is that if you're struggling you need to be open about it and talk to people. I'm still on anti-depressants but now understand it's like having heart disease or asthma. If you need medication to be healthy, why wouldn't you take it? Now I try and spread this message – especially to men who think they can't talk about feeling sad. They think they have to be strong and silent. I tell them that going on anti-depressants and having therapy is the responsible thing to do because you can't be the husband, father or friend you want to be if you're not healthy.'

One of the reasons Daryl is so passionate about telling his story and showing how far he's come is that he knows how many people misunderstand depression and the importance of medication. He was quite surprised when, on his return to South Africa, three of his friends opened up to him about their journeys with mental health. 'They'd been going to therapy and were also on antidepressants. We'd been feeling the same things, but had never spoken about it. This is crazy. The only way we can make it okay for people to open up and get the help they need is for people to start talking about it, which is what I do.

'I discovered SADAG and subscribed to their magazine and newsletter. I'm not sure how they got in touch with me but they asked me to talk at a Mental Health Summit, which I really enjoyed and at which I learnt so much from others. I also talk at schools about mental health and not being frightened about talking about your sexuality. It's not just for those kids who might be gay, but just as much for the bullies, who need to know the impact bullying or ostracisation can have on people. Not just in the short term but that it stays with someone for years and years. Nowadays, with social media, these types of situations are far worse than when I was at school.'

Roelda is only too aware of how difficult it still is for society to let people be open. Living in a small town where you can't walk down the street without bumping into acquaintances, the stigma attached to mental health is palpable.

'I've seen countless times in a workplace situation where people are frightened to say they have problems with depression or bipolar disorder because of the fear they may lose their jobs. Employers are just worried that they don't want people "like that" to work for them. They might take time off, costing money and effort. So people hide their feelings and their problems, not trusting anyone enough to talk about it.

'You get all these fridge magnets with emergency numbers for plumbers, electricians, emergency services, but no suicide helplines. I know now that SADAG does have such a line but if a person wants to take their life that number should be known everywhere.

'Once Daryl got home he heard from a lot of people who told him they'd been in therapy for 15 years and friends who asked why he hadn't shared his problems with them. This has certainly changed my views on the need for mental health education and the importance of mental health professionals.

'People in our small town didn't know where to look when they saw me. They'd quickly turn and walk the other way. Some men wanted to comfort me – others were worried I'd burst into tears. Others simply didn't know what to say. And of course there were some who were simply insensitive.'

For Daryl these days, being in a wheelchair is far easier than working through his depression. 'Each day I'm faced with physical challenges and you have to find a way to solve them, whether it's getting to the bathroom or into a car. You don't have a choice so you figure it out quickly. With the depression I spent so many years pushing it to the back of my mind and ignoring it, that it was really difficult to bring it to the centre and articulate and work through it.

'When I first came back I joined a wheelchair-volleyball team, which I really enjoyed – until I realised their aim was to make the Paralympics, whereas mine was more to socialise.

Although I stopped doing this it really helped with overcoming my disability.

'I've now got a great psychiatrist who I can also talk to about anything as she doubles for me as a therapist and is trained in CBT [cognitive behavioural therapy], which sometimes I feel helps me even more than the meds. It's taught me coping skills and empowered me to deal with this on my own. At the same time she assures me the pills are definitely working because, after all, I'm still here and fine.

'We've lowered my dosage, and although technically I still have depression this doesn't mean I'm not happy. I have a fulfilled life, great relationships and that's still something people don't really understand. You can have depression and still be happy.

'I'm still in marketing and have worked for my company for the last five years, while also studying psychology through UNISA. I finished my honours degree last year and hope to qualify in the next few years.'

To say Daryl fully immerses himself in everything life has to offer is an understatement, with his recent theatre role as testimony to his determination to live life to the fullest. 'My whole outlook has changed now. I'm a lot more outgoing and one of my greatest joys is my singing lessons. I was even in a production of *South Pacific* and am rehearsing for other concerts with my singing teacher.

'I don't have a partner right now – but that's fine. For the first time in my life I'm really happy with who I am and where I'm at.'

'Daryl and I agree that there are probably things we'll never say to each other, not wanting to hurt each other,' Roelda admits. 'We talked a lot when I was with him in England and after he came back, and we have a good relationship. In my heart, though, I suppose I'll always wonder if I couldn't have prevented it.

'I don't think people realise how much courage it took for Daryl to come back to South Africa. He'd always felt suffocated living in a small place like Melkbosstrand, with the small village mentality. He'd always wanted to escape. We'd always thought Daryl was going to do great things and it was hard to see him come back to a place he didn't really want to be. But if there has to be a purpose or something good to come out of this, then it's the fact that he's changing people's perceptions about depression and maybe saving another family from going through what we did.'

TOOLBOX TIPS

Suicide prevention plan

- ❏ Many people with mental health issues think about suicide, but not all want to act on these thoughts. Having a plan for what to do when the urge to act on these thoughts arrives is really helpful to prevent yourself from doing so. You can carry it with you for whenever you need it.
- ❏ Your plan should include:
  - ❏ Several names and contact details of people you trust. The SADAG suicide hotline number (0800 456 789) should be one of them. My3 is a great app for this.
  - ❏ Activities to manage distress – dialectical behaviour therapy (DBT) has good distress tolerance skills.

Google it and find what works for you.

❏ Where to go – identify your local clinic/hospital, church or place where you will be able to find immediate support.

❏ A reminder that you're not alone – there are people who can help; you just have to reach out.

Don't make assumptions

❏ Don't assume people know how you feel or that you know how they feel – you need to speak about it. Mental illnesses affect how we perceive ourselves, others and the world, so it's important to make sure you don't just believe these thoughts as the truth. No one can read minds or help you if they don't know what's going on.

Affirmations

❏ Being left to our own thoughts is often not helpful, especially if they're affected by mental illness. Identify messages of kindness, compassion and/or motivation for yourself that you can be reminded of throughout your day.

Seek help

❏ If you're not feeling mentally and emotionally well, seek help.

Connect

❏ You don't have to do this alone. If you can't connect with friends or family, try finding people who will understand what you're going through – support groups or online communities, for example.

4

SINDI VAN ZYL

Depression

Sindi van Zyl had everything she'd ever wanted: her dream job as a medical doctor, an adoring husband and two beautiful children. But beneath the veneer of success was a woman battling daily with her mental health, afraid to let anyone see her pain. Surprising, you would think, given that she's a medical doctor; it shows how powerful the stigma of mental illness really is.

I first met Sindi when she was a guest speaker at one of our Responsible Reporting on Mental Health workshops for journalists in 2019. I was impressed by how open she was about her journey with mental health, particularly as a practising doctor. Being an extremely warm, outgoing person, she didn't surprise me when she agreed to be part of this book, using her story to reach people to break the stigma – particularly as a black woman.

We meet in a leafy courtyard of a Stanley Avenue restaurant in Johannesburg and she greets me as though we're old friends.

Instead of weighing right in about her illness, I ask her for some background about her life. Born in Harare, Zimbabwe, in 1976, she grew up as a cherished only child in what was initially a single-parent home. Her mom, originally from

KwaZulu-Natal, had moved to Zimbabwe in 1974. A few years later, when her granny, aunt and cousins moved in overnight, the house, explains Sindi, 'became full'.

'One day I suddenly woke up and wasn't an only child any more. This was a good thing as I'd probably have been a spoiled brat,' she laughs. 'I saw how my mom took on the role of nurturer for everyone, which rubbed off on me. I'm also very nurturing and caring, going beyond for people, which has proven to be at my expense.

'Although we weren't rich, my parents, even though divorced, made sure I went to a good private girls' school. My mom had done a lot of work for both the ANC and PAC over the years, so when they asked how they could repay her she immediately had the answer – help towards my daughter's education, which they did, together with my dad. I did well at school and whenever I could I always found myself helping people.

'My first real heartache in life was the usual story. Girl meets boy. Boy breaks girl's heart. I was only 16 and had been thrilled when he agreed to come to our school dance with me. This was it – I thought I was head over heels in love with him. Then suddenly it was over and I was left totally confused and – for the first time, now looking back on it – depressed. He'd dumped me over a school holiday and when I returned to school my best friend couldn't wait to show me the teddy bears and flowers her new boyfriend was sending her. Of course her new boyfriend was my ex-boyfriend. She'd met up with him at a party I didn't go to. I'd actually encouraged them to go together without ever thinking this would happen.' She smiles now as she tells the story but you can tell there was deep hurt at the time. Most parents would put this down as a normal part of growing up – the first heartbreak. Mostly they'd be right, and their child would get over it. But sometimes it grows into a bigger wound.

'It was three weeks into the new school term before I found out who my friend's new boyfriend was and when I did my marks plummeted. The weird thing was none of my teachers even questioned why suddenly this really good student was getting 20 per cent for maths and science. Naturally I failed my A Levels, which just added to my growing depression at the time, especially as I'd had my heart set on studying medicine.'

Her parents were surprised and disappointed by her results and her dad said she'd just have to redo the year, which was something she couldn't even contemplate. 'Can you imagine – at 18 years old seeing all my friends go off to university, leaving me behind to go back to school. I said to him that as a lawyer with lots of connections, including the registrar of the University of Zimbabwe, couldn't he still get me in? He refused point blank and so my mom pointed out to him that the only reason she was still in Zimbabwe was for me and that if this was the case she was moving back to South Africa, which she did.'

This was just the first blow that would see Sindi spiral even further downwards. She found herself having to study again for her A Levels – at night, this time, as the lecturer worked in the day. 'This wasn't the best scenario for me as, apart from a typing course, which ultimately really helped me, I had too much free time on my hands, so found myself drinking, smoking and doing everything I shouldn't have been doing and then going to lectures at night. Everyone in my crowd knew I'd flunked out which made things even worse. Added to which my girlfriend and ex were still dating which was really tough for me. This was my first deep heartbreak and shaped a lot of the bad decisions I'd take going forward. My behaviour was really about numbing the pain I was feeling but I knew it was building up to be an epic disaster, making things worse.' And still those around her didn't see the red flags.

What's becoming more apparent today is the amount of stress matric learners – and, in Sindi's case, A Level students – are under to get the grades they need to get into university. This is an area that both schools and parents need to pay attention to. At that age, kids seem self-assured, but often they're far from it.

Fortunately, a fresh start was on Sindi's horizon. 'Once I'd redone my A Levels – which I managed to pass, although not with the results I'd wanted – I joined my mother in South Africa. My mom was living in Pretoria at the time, in a little apartment in Schoeman Street, downtown Pretoria. I'd applied to the University of Cape Town, which had accepted me for medicine but sadly we couldn't afford it, so there I was sitting at home, listening to the radio and thinking about my life. One day, looking out the window of the flat I saw these young people selling university rag magazines. I wasn't sure what this was as we didn't have rag week in Zimbabwe and I had no idea there was a university on my doorstep. It wasn't until the beginning of March that our landlord Charl told my mom about "the varsity up the road", suggesting we should go there to try and get me in.

'We literally walked up the road and there was the University of Pretoria. We went to the main building and asked where we could apply for me to do medicine. They said I was too late for that but maybe to apply for the BSc at another UP campus down the road. When we got there the dean's secretary said, barely looking up, that applications were closed. She didn't reckon on dealing with my mom, who told her we weren't going to leave until we saw the dean. So we sat and sat and sat, until eventually two hours later she said he'd see us. Unfortunately he had no idea about O Levels or A Level exams, so he gave us the standard "we're full" answer. My mom then turned to me and said in Zulu, "Sindi – I'm not the one who wants to become a medical doctor, you are. I've done my bit. I got you here, now talk to this man and tell him."'

When Sindi tells this story you can hear her mother's voice coming through and I begin to realise where a lot of Sindi's strength and personality come from. She explained to the dean that A Levels were equivalent to first-year university in South Africa and assured him that if he let her in she'd catch up. Her argument was persuasive and he agreed.

'The following week, now 20 years old, I waltzed into this class, where no one had ever seen me before, and I even got a room in the famous Huis Erika residence. I'd told them I wanted to become a doctor and they suggested I apply to every intake for medicine and not give up. They also suggested I change my subjects to BSc physiology and psychology in case I don't become a doctor, which I did in my second year.

'A slight hindrance was my complete lack of Afrikaans but luckily the head of physiology, Professor Viljoen, was our lecturer and she was fascinated by this black Zimbabwean girl, so each day when I got to class she'd say, "Goeie môre," and give me an Afrikaans lesson. This was how I learnt Afrikaans, and as my main subject was in this language, this was essential. At first I paid people to translate my text books, then after a while I got an Afrikaans/English dictionary which really helped.' Given Sindi's determination to succeed, it's not surprising that she'd add learning a language to her already-full academic schedule.

'One day I saw a notice about auditioning for Radio Tuks, the university's radio station, so I went along and applied to be a newsreader. I went back the following day and looked at the list pinned to the noticeboard with the names of the successful applicants. I was devastated when I didn't see my name there, until someone said, "Your name is on the DJ list," and suddenly there I was – DJ Sindz, the first black female radio disc jockey in the university's history. I did this for the next five years and loved it,' she says, laughing and giving me an arm-wave demonstration of her DJ look.

Each year she'd apply for medicine, but it was only in her fourth and final year of her BSc that she got accepted. 'I did this without getting any credits for my BSc, meaning I had to start from scratch, but I thought, *My dream has to come true*. The only downside was once again I found myself coming out of a very messy relationship just as I was going into medical studies which didn't help ease me into my first year. Once again my bad behaviour, drinking, smoking and too much partying that goes with hard student life, came into play. It was my way of dealing, once again, with my depression. When you're depressed you find things to fill that hole. And of course I wasn't acknowledging this as depression.'

This is common behaviour, particularly for someone like Sindi who would be classed as high-functioning. She wants to be open as she can about it, despite her high profile in her field, sparing nothing in her quest to help others.

'Luckily in my second year of medicine I joined a church, was born again and found Jesus, which literally saved me. The news spread like wildfire – "You know Sindi, the wild one, she's now born again" – everyone was shocked. It was a complete transformation. The other good thing that happened that year was meeting my wonderful husband Marinus van Zyl, who volunteered to transport people to and from the church I attended. 2001 – what a year; I went from a wild child to a born-again Christian, and met my white Afrikaans husband,' she laughs.

'I was very happy and there was also a lot of forgiveness in my life and repairing of relationships. Three years later Marinus and I got married and when I graduated the following year I decided I wanted to do my internship in Soweto and give my heart and passion to working with black people. So I applied to Baragwanath Hospital [now the Chris Hani Baragwanath Hospital]. I speak Zulu and Shona, as well as Tswana, which I learnt while living in Pretoria. Not many interns volunteered to go to Bara so I was pleased to get in but had no idea what I was in for. There was nothing on earth that could possibly have prepared me for the death and despair that HIV was causing then, in 2005.'

Hospitals were neither prepared for nor trained to deal with the number of HIV/Aids cases and the deaths this virus brought with it. For Sindi and many other young doctors at the time, this was particularly challenging – and beyond stressful, the reality of HIV pushing her further down into the depths of depression.

'When today you see graphs showing the peak of the deaths caused by HIV, it was around 2006/7 – while I was at Bara. When I first arrived I started off in paediatrics. Babies were dying like flies and I wasn't coping. My second rotation was internal medicine and as it was winter we knew that for people with HIV and weak chests this would be particularly hard.

74

When I try to explain to people this situation words are never enough. I soon started smoking again, in a constant state of worry about my patients. I was so determined to save lives. I was one of those doctors who, when I arrived at work to find a patient had died, I'd start sobbing. I'd go to bed at night thinking when I get there tomorrow we'll do bloods but when I arrived and asked where that patient was, the nurses would flippantly say, "Oh, she's gone." It broke my heart.' She still chokes up at the memory.

'There would be five of us on call, four on the ward admitting patients and one who was on ward call. This is the person who gets called when a patient, for instance, is having a fit or if a patient passes away. So on any given night during ward call I was certifying about 25 bodies a night. We would take turns doing the different duties between casualty admitting and being on call in the ward. When a patient died the nurses would wrap the body and get a death certificate ready, put it in a file which they'd put to one side. They'd call me whatever time of night it was to certify the deaths before calling the mortuary to fetch all the bodies.

'Sometimes I'd arrive on the ward to find they'd wrapped ten bodies before I'd had a chance to even certify them as dead. I'd make the nurses unwrap each body to confirm they were dead which the nurses hated me for. They'd say, "Oh, it's Van Zyl and you know what she'll make us do." I'd only sign the death certificate when I'd confirmed the death. I understood they were overwhelmed but somehow they became callous with it. I felt you can't let your integrity and your standards drop. Maybe I did also in some areas of my life but not when it came to my patients and people's lives. You can falter in your own life but not when it comes to other people.

'I seemed to be constantly in tears. I was putting my all into my work which is where my later passion for working with HIV cases came from. It wasn't a conscious decision at the time. I just think seeing all those babies dying in paediatrics and the adults in medicine broke me. But the worst was still to come.'

The waiter arrives with our breakfast. His timing is perfect; it gives Sindi a moment to take a breath before carrying on with the story.

'Next I moved to surgery and here I worked with a doctor from Eastern Europe. He'd been at Bara for a long time but had kept failing his exams. He had a principle that he wouldn't operate on a patient until he had their HIV test results, which back then took five hours. I was totally against this practice but I was just an intern and had no say. One day, a lady in her 50s came in with an acute abdomen problem so we rushed her to theatre. But this doctor said no, he wouldn't touch her until he had her HIV test results. I went home and the next morning on ward rounds when we reached her bed I asked where she was. This was in front of professors, senior registrars, everyone. The nurse calmly replied, "She died." Right there and then I lost it – in front of everyone. I told the doctor he had killed that patient with his HIV test rules, and then, crying, I fled the ward.

'My experiences at Bara formed me. Something happened there that shifted the core of who I was and would become. Although my husband has always been a good listener, it was easier to come home and drink than talk, so I was always drinking. I felt that everyone's going through this – I'm not special, so I don't need to see a therapist. Bara is tough but I must get through it. Obviously, looking back, I should have gone to see someone. Even today the hospitals need to change the way they work, particularly with interns. It's not okay to work 36 hours straight.'

A massive problem for many young doctors is the long hours and pressures of working in underfunded, poorly resourced hospitals. For Sindi, with her undiagnosed and untreated depression, and as in many similar cases, alcohol was the easy answer.

'When I got home I'd go straight for my coping mechanism – a few bottles of Hunter's Dry. I still managed to go to church – my love of God didn't change and I tried, given the circumstances, my best to be a good wife. We were also trying to have a baby but I don't think the drinking helped.'

Today, doctors and nurses are still crying out to be heard, particularly student doctors. What is noticeable, though, is the increase in the number of suicides in this particular group. Something desperately needs to change. Sindi is insistent about one thing: these young doctors mustn't be afraid to get help. They are not expected to be perfect.

After her internship, Sindi went to Coronation Hospital, part of the Helen Joseph complex, which she found less frantic and better than Bara. Once again she found herself in the paediatric ward, as well as in orthopaedics.

'I also worked at community clinics, which is where I fell back in love with medicine. By the end of 2007 I decided to work at Meadowlands Clinic in Soweto where I stayed for a year, doing my overtime at Lilian Ngoyi Community Clinic and in Lenasia South. My work was now so much more satisfying.

'In February 2008 I finally fell pregnant and my daughter Nandi was born in October.' We pause the interview while the proud mom shows me some photos of her children.

'I stayed home on maternity leave for a while and then returned to Meadowlands. At the same time an NGO based in

Soweto working in the HIV / Aids field heard about me and my work ethic, and offered me a job, which I took. This was very fulfilling as I finally felt I was really doing something towards making sure no one would die the way they had in 2006. By then medication was more readily available but the issue now was coping with the growing waiting lists.'

Sindi's new job was an exercise in changing hearts and minds. 'Our job was to train nurses in dealing with HIV / Aids and patient care. They were scared, with some not even wanting to do it. Our job was to explain HIV in simple terms to get the nurses to understand and be able to give the treatment, especially for pregnant women. This was extremely important as there were still a lot of babies being born with HIV, which we desperately wanted to change. The prevention of mother-to-baby transmission was our priority. I used to say to the nurses: "The adults can take care of themselves but an HIV baby is fully reliant on another adult to make sure their medication is taken – they can't take it themselves. They must still grow up to go to crèche, primary school, high school – all while living with HIV."

'Winning them over wasn't easy. They felt they were already burdened with a lot of work and we found the way to get through to them was storytelling. I'd tell them stories about Bara and the number of babies who had died. I'd say some of you are already grannies and if you don't implement this programme for these pregnant mothers, they're going to give birth to HIV-positive babies who will grow up and fall in love with your grandchildren. They don't know if they're HIV positive because no one will check. So how will you feel if your grandchild one day becomes HIV positive because you refused to treat a lady to save her baby from being infected? I even appealed to their blackness and their spirit of Ubuntu to make them do the right thing.

'Some clinics would have 40 women arrive who would be told that only 20 of them could be seen. The rest must go home. For each day they didn't know their status it was an extra day not knowing whether their babies were infected. It was so hard and I couldn't understand why they couldn't see it.'

Sindi was dealing with all the stresses of her job, much of which she would take home with her. Having a young child didn't make life easier. She was on the edge, and she didn't know it. Help was so near but she still wasn't ready to go there.

'In 2011 I joined Twitter and it saved my life,' explains Sindi in a voice that tells me how excited she was to find social media. 'At first I'd complain about my work and all the challenges. One day someone said, "Sindi, it can't be that you're always complaining about your work, why don't you rather use this platform to educate us so we can share the information and help people understand what needs to be done." That was a real lightbulb moment for me. Then I started writing a blog on another guy's site, which had a big following. On Twitter I'd give nuggets of information and advice – #HIV, #thisisforever, and so on. I'd tell them what to do and people started sharing this information.

'When people asked me about this I'd say if the health system can't do the right things, let the patient force the right thing out of the health system. When a patient comes in and looks like they know their rights, they get treated very differently from a patient who doesn't. White patients fell into that category whereas black patients simply wouldn't complain. My tweets and blogging I called active citizenship. Empowering people to force their healthcare workers to do the right thing ultimately saved my life. A lot of the pain and pressure I'd been feeling over the years lifted once I joined Twitter and realised that through this powerful platform I could save lives. That really changed my life and still does to this day.'

In the same year as Sindi started tweeting, she fell pregnant again and had her son Marinus, named after his father, in the December. What she didn't know during her pregnancy was that she had preeclampsia, a complication characterised by high blood pressure with a possibility of damage to the liver and kidneys.

'By around eight months I knew I was putting on quite a bit of weight but thought it was the pregnancy. One day a nurse I was training looked at me and said, "Doctor, you're not looking good, you're very puffy." I explained I was pregnant but she insisted on testing my urine and blood pressure, which was through the roof. My husband rushed to the clinic and took me straight to hospital.

'The timing couldn't have been worse because as I got to the hospital my friends were gathered at a Milpark restaurant for my baby shower – without me. I wasn't able to contact everyone so I was getting messages asking where I was. I was angry at myself – a doctor – for having this diagnosis and not knowing I was sick.

'Marinus was born with the cord around his neck and was rushed straight to ICU. This also made me angry. I was angry at everything. I went on maternity leave and stayed home for a while but by then all the things that went wrong around his birth pushed me towards my final breakdown. I also had postpartum depression, which no one picked up. Again I questioned myself – how could I be depressed? I had a boy – what our whole family had dreamed about, especially with eight granddaughters. But I just wasn't truly happy.'

It would be expected that husbands and family may not identify postpartum depression – but even though Sindi is a doctor herself, neither she nor the medical professionals around her noticed anything. This is an extremely common condition, which often goes undiagnosed and can grow into a serious mental health condition.

Sindi's voice joins the voices in almost every interview in this book when she tells me, 'I didn't think this could be depression with everything I had to be thankful for.' Generally, when women are pregnant they hear all about what to do with their baby – from changing nappies to breastfeeding to nutrition – but rarely does anyone mention postpartum depression.

'The months went by and I returned to work and by the following June I started changing. Formerly a social butterfly, now I wasn't even eating. I was weepy and I was sinking. I didn't want to see anyone.' This is hard to imagine of the larger-than-life, supremely confident woman sitting opposite me.

'One day in 2013 I suddenly woke up and said to my friends, "I think I'm depressed." Their reaction was to tell me to stop being so dramatic. My husband knew something was wrong but didn't know what to do either. In February they fired my boss and made me a manager. The worst thing you can do to a person like me is take me away from my patients and give me time sheets, budgets and admin work.

'To compound the depression I went to work one morning only to come back that night and find our apartment empty. My husband had decided it was time for us to move but hadn't told me. During the day he'd got his friends to come and they moved our entire home. This plus my change at work was just too much for me. I even missed my best friend's wedding. I got up that day, dressed for the wedding and then, not being able to face it, went straight back to bed. I'd really deteriorated. Suddenly every single noise would put my nerves on edge, which I didn't know then was something called hyperacusis. Our bedroom was very close to the main road so I moved to the guest room, put earplugs in my ears but could still acutely hear noise.

'Each night at around 4am my baby son would wake for a nappy change. One night, with my husband fast asleep next to me, I heard my son rattling his cot. I knew what was wrong and that I needed to change his nappy but I couldn't move. I just lay there and cried and cried. The next morning I called a doctor friend of mine who had told me her story of depression the previous year. I told her what was happening and she said I needed to call my doctor and tell him what was going on. He arrived at the house, asked me a few questions and said, "You've got clinical depression and you need to get help now." I'd known this in my heart for a long time but no one would believe me, particularly because I'm really good at running on autopilot. My doctor arranged for me to be admitted to hospital straight away and the one thing I asked was that no one told my mother until everything was arranged.'

There's suddenly a word here that wasn't in Sindi's story before – 'clinical' depression, meaning that this is a clinical illness that affects the brain, just as having a heart condition affects the heart or diabetes affects glucose levels. This was a word Sindi knew only too well and what finally convinced her that she needed to do what the mental health professionals were telling her to do.

'When my mom and aunt did come to the hospital I could see my mom wasn't happy. I told them everything and being religious Christians they laid hands on me and did what they thought would help, which is great because God does heal, but I needed to be in hospital. My mom didn't understand and asked me why was I in this place with all these people – in a mental health hospital. By then I was on medication and I looked at her and said, "I'm not well so I have to be here."

'Over the next three weeks she only saw me twice as it was hard for her to see me there. For her, mental health carried a stigma, which it does for so many people. She was so worried what people would think, she swore me to secrecy so no one would know where I was. When I came home I could see she was ashamed. She had a whole load of reasons I shouldn't be depressed. After all, I was married to a great husband, had two beautiful children and was a doctor. What hadn't she done for me? She'd dedicated her life for me. She saw my breakdown and depression as her failure. How could I be depressed when I had so much?'

Families often ask themselves, when a family member develops mental health issues, what they could have done differently. Ultimately, only the person living with the illness themselves can start the process of getting better, particularly in the case of clinical depression.

'Being in hospital was like heaven for me. I was the patient being looked after and I could just let go. I loved the art sessions and the knitting. I loved everything about the experience, particularly having no responsibilities. I could just be me and it was the most healing thing. Of course, by then I was also on antidepressants and having therapy. I found it fascinating that by sitting and telling my story, I saw this amazing psychologist take the threads and weave them into ropes, piecing everything together.'

You would imagine that, as a doctor herself, Sindi would understand the value of psychology – but if you ask a medical doctor how much they learnt about therapy in medical school, you'll find it's a minimal amount.

I can hear the relief in Sindi's voice as she continues her story. 'During therapy I was able to talk about all the things that had happened during my internship and community service. One of the things my psychologist said was that I had to forgive myself, which really helped me. Once I came out of hospital I was given some time off and I could feel I was getting better and working on myself also.'

But Sindi was soon to face her worst nightmare. 'Just seven weeks after my hospital admission, on the 22nd of May, my mom died. I was shattered – my mom meant the whole world to me. Even my psychiatrist was lost for words, as these two traumatic events in my life had happened so close together. I knew my breakdown had been really difficult for my mom, added to which she was a diabetic. It all happened so fast: she became sick on a Thursday and died the following Wednesday, in ICU on a ventilator.

'My psychiatrist decided to add to my medication because my depression went from being about me and my healing to being about my mom's death. Grief and depression are two different things. I was battling to understand why my mom had gone and it was hell. Thank goodness I was on medication when she died because I'm not sure what I would have done otherwise. I believe God prepares us for these things and my being on medication did just that.

'After the cremation I kept my mom's ashes in a box in my wardrobe as I wasn't ready for her to be interred. I also told God I wanted her to come back. It says in the Bible, Ezekiel 37:

"You are able to raise the bones and put them together with the flesh and skin." Every morning I'd wake up and say to God, I'm still waiting for you to bring my mom back. But He didn't and that was hard.

'I eventually stopped working at the NGO in July 2014 and took the rest of the year off, before going back in March 2015. I was tired and even felt I didn't want to be a doctor any more, which wasn't a practical thing financially. I felt like saying I'm done and hanging up my stethoscope. But instead for the next two years I worked at a clinic in downtown Johannesburg, which I did enjoy, before moving to where I am now, in private practice.' It was a new start for Sindi.

'It was only at the end of 2016 that I felt ready to let go of my mom's ashes.' Tears form in her eyes. 'I woke up one day, sat in front of my wardrobe and told God to bring her back. My husband came to sit next to me and said, "Honey, you need to give the ashes to your family because you know she's not coming back." I cried, but understood, and gave them over to the family, and we interred them. This was really hard but I was still on medication, which kept me hanging in there. I was also still going to therapy – just not as often as before and, importantly, I was getting better.

'One of the biggest changes I had to make was learning to have boundaries, accepting that I can't save the world. This was hard for me to accept – that I must deal with one person at a time and couldn't help everyone at the same time. The cognitive behavioural therapy I did with my psychologist really helped, teaching me how to react in situations: to look at a situation, assess its severity and, on a scale from one to ten, judge how bad it is and how I should react. I had to learn all these things as I wasn't naturally like that.'

Cognitive behavioural therapy (CBT) is a highly effective and popular talking therapy that manages people's problems by changing the way they think and behave.

'Navigating the grief was the hardest thing for me and I was now a completely different person to the one I'd been before. Suddenly I wasn't afraid of anything. Suddenly getting through the day became much easier. I wasn't waking up feeling tired and not coping. This whole experience also completely changed my attitude towards mental illness.

'I realised that, throughout all my studies at medical school, mental health was barely touched on. We're not sensitised enough, which is why medical students and doctors would rather keep it all to themselves than share when they have a problem. You hear someone is depressed, someone has taken their own life, but what does this mean? There were two members of my family who died by suicide and you understand, but don't really understand. You think there should have been a better solution for this person. Maybe they could have done this or that or maybe they still would have done what they did. Until you've walked in those shoes and heard those voices telling you you'd be better off dead, you can't understand.' I can hear the passion in her voice and, at the same time, the frustration that more people don't know this.

'When Robin Williams, one of my favourite actors, died by suicide in August 2014 I decided it was time for me to speak out. I thought if I could tell my story and tell one person to not die by suicide, I'm going to. I called my dad, as he was coming to South Africa the following week, and said, "I need to talk to you. I need to tell you a story because I'm going to do something but I wouldn't want you to find out in the newspapers." Because my mom didn't want me to tell anyone, he didn't know

86

about my breakdown the previous year, so I explained what had happened to me and that I wanted to speak out. I wanted to help save lives, not with medicine this time but by talking about my experience. I said that as a doctor with an established following on social media around HIV/Aids, I thought I was in a good position to do this. Added to which being a Christian was important, because Christianity didn't always accommodate mental illness. I told him I felt I had work to do and he said, "Fine, go ahead." So that was it – I wrote a blog on my experiences and have been tweeting ever since. SADAG saw what I was doing, reached out to me and I've been one of their advocates ever since.'

When people like Sindi speak out, it makes the world of difference in breaking down the stigma of mental health, particularly in the black community.

At last, Sindi started to feel the lightness of life. 'These days I'm a busy, although probably a little unconventional, working mom, with a 12-year-old daughter and 9-year-old son. Both kids are very close to their dad, particularly because during their early years when I was absent from their lives with my depression, retreating to my bed so much, they came to rely on him.

'What really brought me back to life was a dream trip to New York. In September 2017 I was invited by the Gates Foundation as part of a group to attend an event there. It was a fully paid trip and my long-cherished dream of visiting the Big Apple came true. When things weren't going well for me I always thought, it doesn't matter, one day I'll get to go to New York. Then my mom died and I thought, *My worst nightmare has happened, now nothing else is going to go right*, so I just gave up on the New York dream. 'Being there was unbelievable. I remember standing in Times Square at midnight with all those lights surrounding me, thinking if New York could happen in a way I didn't expect, then it means I need to continue with my life. When I return home I'm going to carry on with everything I've put on hold. All the dreams I had need to be reignited.

'Today I'm able to be a better mother to Nandi and Marni and wife to my wonderful husband Marinus and every year now I go back to New York …'

TOOLBOX TIPS

Family support

- ❏ Family members struggling with guilt, anger or worry about why their loved one is ill should seek their own support.
- ❏ It's not helpful to focus on the past and how things should have been done differently.
- ❏ Get support and educate yourself, so that you can be there for the family member who needs you.

Seek professional care

- ❏ Being admitted to a psychiatric facility comes with a lot of stigma. What many don't realise is how helpful it can be.
- ❏ Just as you would go to hospital to treat a physical illness, you should go to a psychiatric facility if you're not coping with your mental health.
- ❏ In hospital, you're treated by a multidisciplinary team of professionals, all there to help you gain skills to cope.

Compassion for yourself

❑ People focus a lot of attention on past decisions, mistakes or regrets, berating themselves for things they cannot change. This isn't helpful.

❑ What *is* helpful is to be patient, kind and compassionate with yourself. Forgive yourself as you would others, and bring your attention to the present moment.

One step at a time

❑ It's easy to become overwhelmed when expecting too much from yourself. Be realistic. Set reachable goals. Set boundaries for yourself and others. Do one thing at a time.

❑ Focus on what you're doing, in the moment, instead of focusing on all the things that need to be done.

Create space in your life for yourself

❑ People mistakenly think they'll take a break when everything that needs to be done is done. But to-do lists are never-ending, leaving many exhausted and overwhelmed.

❑ Taking breaks, mentally and physically, where you feel fulfilled is important. The more replenished you feel, the easier life becomes.

❑ Identify activities you enjoy and carve out time for them – even if it's just a dedicated 10 to 15 minutes a day that's purely for you.

5

SIPHO SIMELANE

Suicide attempts

Try something for me.

Set the alarm on your phone to go off every 40 seconds. Every time you hear that sound, it represents someone, somewhere, in the world who has taken his or her life.

According to the World Health Organization's *Global Health Estimates 2016* report, South Africa's estimated suicide rate of 12 people per 100 000 is approximately four times the global rate of 3.6 per 100 000. It's hard to imagine such figures being reality, but when you hear that last year SADAG received 145 000 calls to its 22 helplines it puts these figures into perspective.

Although more men than women die from suicide, this is mainly because men use more aggressive methods such as guns or hanging. Women generally swallow pills or poison. So the question remains: How do we change these horrific statistics? Allowing people not only to talk about their stresses, anxiety and depression but also to be heard and understood would go a long way towards helping to achieve this.

In a 2019 press release, the WHO suggests 'restricting access to means; educating the media on responsible reporting of suicide; implementing programmes among young people to build life skills that enable them to cope with life stresses; and early identification, management and follow-up of people at risk of suicide' (to read the full text, see https://www.who.int/news-room/detail/09-09-2019-suicide-one-person-dies-every-40-seconds). To this end, I assist SADAG in holding regular sessions with the media about responsible reporting on mental health. We need people to understand – and, above all, recognise – the signs that someone close to them, a colleague or an employee is in real need of help.

Sipho Simelane's story in particular illustrates how hard it sometimes is to know how someone is feeling. On the surface he seemed fine but in reality he was suffering so badly that there was no light to be seen in his future.

Sipho Simelane looks as though he has it all. He's an extremely successful businessman, international traveller, husband to beautiful wife Disemelo, and father to three handsome boys, Bohlale, Sihle and Thandowenkosi. But on 17 August 2011 he tried not once but three times to take his life – and failed: a failure that, today, he's very grateful for.

I heard about Sipho through SADAG. He'd come forward to help destigmatise mental health and get people to understand what a suicide attempt means, particularly in some black communities. Mental illness is seen differently in many cultures, but in many black communities it's often linked to having been cursed by an enemy or having done something to displease the ancestors, among other things. With media and other interventions, this mindset is slowly shifting to encompass the medical reality that clinical depression is a real illness and needs real medicine.

I meet Sipho at an upmarket Melrose coffee shop where it's apparent to me that he's a regular – he's greeted by management and the waiters as he makes his way over to me with a

wide smile on his face. Sipho is one of those people you'd definitely pick out in a crowd with his trademark way of dressing
and snazzy hats. He wouldn't look out of place with a saxo-
phone in his hands at a New York jazz club. He greets me with
a warm hug and we chat a little before we start on his remarkable story. If I didn't know a little of what I was about to hear,
I would never in a million years think that this was someone
who would contemplate taking his life. I ask him to take me
back to his childhood to see if I can find any signs of what was
to come.

Sipho was born in 1970 and grew up running free in the
township of Daveyton, on what was known then as the East
Rand. Words such as 'stress', 'anxiety' and 'depression' were
unheard of in his family: 'I can look back as far as my memory
takes me and say I had a happy, normal childhood, with no real
issues to worry about. People talk about poverty and depriva-
tion in their youth. For me, my siblings and friends, we never
knew the word "poverty". There was always food on the table
and we were properly clothed for school. I don't remember
a lack of anything. In those days we had great freedom and
were happy playing in the streets of our neighbourhood,' he
explains, smiling warmly at the memory.

But those halcyon days didn't last. By the time Sipho was
14, in 1984, things were really hotting up politically in the
country. When his older brother left for Swaziland, his political
awareness was born. Suddenly, he had a lot of questions.

'I also had lots of opinions and was what my father called a
hothead. To keep me safe, my father sent me to live in Umlazi
in KwaZulu-Natal, with a family friend who was a pastor. Here
I quickly became part of their large, lively family and church
community, which protected me from what was happening

around me – the fighting between the Inkatha and UDF [United Democratic Front] parties in the area. This was still in the era when the ANC was a banned organisation.

'Being a church family, there was always music in the house, with people playing drums, guitars and singing. The family were friends with the legendary theatre producer Mbongeni Ngema, so when they announced auditions for his now world-famous production *Sarafina* we all went to try out. Four of my KZN family were part of that first group of performers, who were not only in the South African production but went on to the New York show, with two still performing in *The Lion King* in New York. Although I only played a backstage role, at 16 this opened up a whole new world for me and was an incredible experience.'

You're probably thinking, *How did this guy end up with a rope around his neck?* His life seemed pretty good. At that time he didn't think he had any real problems, but when he analysed that period he saw difficult times that indeed had a lasting impact.

His voice turns serious. 'Simply moving home and schools and finding myself in a completely different world was really hard. When I became involved with *Sarafina*, we didn't look at it as simply theatre. For us, it was protest theatre. We were portraying what we were seeing around us. Friends being arrested and shot, hacked to death in the streets of Umlazi. For us, we weren't just reading about people being butchered. We were *seeing* these things. They were our lived experiences and at the time, not even knowing about post-traumatic stress, I just took these events as part of life. To be lived and then moved on from. Seeking help to talk about these events wasn't part of who we were in this community. No one spoke about it. Everything remained buried inside.

'To this day I don't know if any of the people around me then in my adoptive family or community were affected by these events. No one spoke about it then or since that I know of.'

The impact of living through these frightening, violent times quite possibly left Sipho with undiagnosed and untreated post-traumatic stress disorder (PTSD), which would have built up over a period of time and eventually led to his suicide attempts. People often downplay the effects of even a single violent incident in their lives, which, without intervention, can have long-term effects.

When Sipho left school he returned to his family. The fact that he didn't study further was no deterrent to him and his ambition – his 20s saw him slowly climbing the corporate ladder, working in senior positions in top JSE-listed companies. He always had one eye open, looking for every entrepreneurial opportunity that came his way. In 2004 he thought his luck couldn't get any better when he met Disemelo, the love of his life.

'We soon went into business together and pretty soon had three fast-food outlets in the Eastern Cape.' Not being satisfied with just these, with a friend he began bottling water in Franschhoek, which he then sold nationally through major supermarket outlets. 'Life was good. We moved to East London and within six years had our three boys. Every two years I'd take the family to the United States, visiting famous landmarks such as Disneyland and generally enjoying life.

'The fact I was working all hours, virtually seven days a week, was just part of the deal, I thought. It's what people do and I must get on with it. When I felt it was becoming too much I'd read a motivational book or go to church. I could always spring back from bad days. There was never a day I'd say I can't carry on tomorrow. Until there was ...'

A question many people ask when reading about suicide is, 'How does this happen overnight – going from living your normal life to deciding to take your life?' Sipho almost reads my mind here and explains. 'For about a day and a half this feeling of desperately needing to rest began building inside me. It was hard to verbalise. The nearest explanation I can give is that I wanted to close my eyes and not wake up. I felt so tired but felt there was nobody to talk to, even though I was surrounded by my wonderful wife and family. Although I considered myself worldly wise and educated, maybe my culture was kicking in. I'd read about depression but perhaps wasn't able to identify it or understand how to seek help. For those two days I didn't even think I could get help.'

If Sipho's house had caught fire or he'd been in an accident, he'd call the fire brigade or an ambulance without even thinking – but when it comes to mental illness, who do you call?

'When I've been asked about my suicide attempt I'd say it's about a feeling you have. It's not about hurting anyone or not caring. You have all the love in the world for your family, friends and life itself. No one had done anything particularly harmful or hurtful to me. Speaking to the psychiatrist made me wonder whether there was some unconscious trigger that sent me over the cliff that day. I still don't know.

'The night before I left home was like any other night. There were no fights, no domestic issues – but I knew exactly what I was going to do the next day. You could have promised me a million dollars and I wouldn't have changed my mind. I just wanted to check out. To have an infinite rest but somehow not thinking I'm going to kill myself. I was overwhelmed with a heavy sadness which is almost impossible to describe, it's so overwhelming. But for all this I knew exactly what I was going

95

to do come the next morning.'

I'm surprised how calm Sipho is as he tells this story, but I understand that for Sipho, as for countless others who have been down the same road, there was no going back. He'd made a decision and all that occupied his mind was carrying this out. Had someone close to him been able to pick up any signs of what he was planning, intervention may have been possible.

But the day came that changed everything. 'On Friday 17 July 2011, after sleeping for less than two hours, I found myself hearing voices in my head debating and planning a perfect suicide which would make headlines on CNN, BBC, SABC and 702 Talk Radio. Award-winning broadcasters Piers Morgan and Richard Quest would be covering the story and tweeting at the same time about it. I pictured my beautiful wife invited to accept awards on this gripping story, followed by an Academy Award for the movie based on the book. I even heard the acceptance speech my wife would give with my boys by her side: "We just don't understand. He was such a strong man. It took everyone by surprise that my husband and father to our boys tried to commit suicide three times in one night. He didn't seem like a guy who would do such a thing."

'But that day I was that guy. On this very cold day I was the first one up, which worked with my "perfect getaway" – ukubaleka. People have often asked me to recall that day and what thoughts I had in my fragile mind. The demons in my head and their huge army had completely taken over my brain and functionality. I'd lost control of my sane faculties. This is what a psychologist later told me during a consultation. I had reached acute depression, which made it difficult to engage on any kind of normal level. My energy levels and faculties had been badly affected and compromised. Depression, stress and anxiety had crept up on me, taking hold of my dreams, thoughts, muscles, movement and my entire world as I knew it. I'd made the decision to end my sad and sorry life as I saw it that day.'

For the first time since sitting down with him, I see sadness cross Sipho's face as I wait for him to continue, almost holding my breath so as not to interrupt his thoughts.

'It was 4 am when I left home with the temperature at minus two degrees Celsius, but even though it was freezing I was sweating in the deep south of Johannesburg where we lived. As I got out of bed I accidentally touched my sweet, lovely wife. I tried not to look at her, so as not to confuse my already muddled mind, and hoped she wouldn't wake up and call me back to bed – or ask what the rush was. That would have changed my plan or completely spoiled it.'

Quietly Sipho changed into a pair of jeans, and his favourite leather jacket and Puma sneakers. He took two pairs of black socks and two T-shirts, all of which he put on as he didn't want to carry any luggage. Grabbing his ID book, passport, driver's licence and medical-aid information, he was ready to leave – and never return.

'This may all sound strange for a man planning to die but somehow in my mind there was obviously a plan where I'd need the best private medical attention en route to my death. Even though this was funny, I definitely didn't laugh right then. I wasn't planning on driving a car but still took my licence. The passport was critical because my escape route included going via Swaziland, my ancestral home and father's birthplace where I planned to end my life.

'I also checked to see I had my bank card as I'd need money for transport and food. There were some sensible thought processes in place as I managed to make myself a double cappuccino and pour it into my travel mug to keep me warm while I walked to the local train station. I left a brief note for my wife: *Gone for a short walk, please don't look for me. Love you lots – Sipho.* Somehow I thought this would stop her panicking in the short term. I left my two mobile phones charging to make it seem normal and also to make sure I wasn't bothered by ringing phones.'

Despite what many people feel after a family member's suicide – that it was a cowardly or selfish act – what they generally don't understand is that for the person taking his or her own life it is the only option. In fact, they would very likely have done it sooner, but had been hanging on for their family's sake. But there comes a moment when they can't hang on any longer. This was Sipho's moment.

There was still a long journey ahead for Sipho as he sat nervously waiting at the railway station. Five trains came on the opposite track – not going in the direction he wanted. 'This was devastating for me as every second counted and I didn't want anyone to find me and haul me back home with my tail between my legs. I was rushing to kill myself.

'After three long hours a train to Springs arrived and I jumped on. Springs was where I would catch a taxi to Swaziland – my end destination. I hadn't shaved for more than two days by then and felt scruffy. I've always been well groomed and so, finding a makeshift barber under a tent, I convinced him to shave my head bald and trim my moustache. I wanted to be a perfect, neat corpse when I was found after my suicide. My grandmother Ma-Ntuli instilled fear and discipline about looking great every time we left home and not embarrassing her in the neighbourhood. Some things stick even in the direst of situations.'

Here and there Sipho injects humour into the narrative. He's a born storyteller who has you hanging on his every word.

'I also ate pap and chicken from the taxi rank, which was going to be the last meal before my death. I didn't want to die hungry or starved, I told the voices in my head. Again it was hurry up and wait as the taxi wouldn't leave until it was full, which turned out to be two and a half hours later – just after midday.

'When we reached Mahamba Border Post, a lady helped me get a lift 25 kilometres into Swaziland. By then it was after 9 am and I wished I'd thought of bringing some whisky or cheap wine to keep me warm. By the time I reached my destination it was dark but I could see the white church next to our village – and eventually, 12 hours after leaving home, I reached my aunt's place, screamed my lungs out, begging and announcing all the clan names to be recognised and for her to wake up to let me put my head down.

'I awoke to the sounds of the first hen trumpeting the day's arrival. My astonished aunt informed me that my arrival in the middle of the night brought out all the neighbours who were involved in crime committees. I left my aunt with money and a small gift, which is what you do in these rural areas, and left as fast as I could before any of the elders could question me around the purpose of my visit.

'My next short stop that Saturday 18 July was to another village and another aunt who I was really close to. I tried my best to look normal, arriving with a box of Kentucky Fried Chicken to announce my visit. Now my mission was getting closer, and a nearby building-supplies store supplied the equipment I'd need – a ten-metre-long rope of a particular strength, which I hid under my jacket as I returned once more to my aunt's house where she'd planned a feast for me. That night I excused myself as they sat around a very tempting fire telling old family stories and jokes.'

Not wanting to hang around the family too long and give anything away, Sipho had his cousin drop him at the local taxi rank, which would carry him to his final destination some 45 kilometres away – where his hanging would take place. 'As the taxi was leaving I started to plan my hanging ritual, the actual moment and the last step. I wasn't scared at all. I was calm and totally ready to meet my maker and end my misery and unworthy self. Every time I saw a perfect tree I wanted to jump out of the taxi, hide and wait for nightfall.

'When the taxi stopped in Manzini I spotted another fast-food outlet and ordered a quarter chicken, roll and chips with a 500 ml can of cold drink. So yes, now my third final meal … After downing the food, my dilemma on this Sunday morning was where to find alcohol. I knew there had to be an illegal shebeen nearby and before long I had a nip [330ml] bottle of no-name brandy to pour into my can of cold drink.

'After another wait for the taxi to fill I arrived at my final destination (literally and figuratively) at 8 at night to find a tree and hang myself. At the border post they stamped my passport and I remember thinking, *Thank goodness they haven't got one of those machines that measures body temperatures*, as I was sweating. Half an hour later I found a slipway into a nearby game reserve. The alcohol had kicked in and any fear I had seeped out. I saw a massive sign on the barbed-wire fence warning people about the presence of the Big Five and that you shouldn't stop anywhere for the next few kilometres. That didn't even concern me.

'Then I spotted a railway line and my heart skipped a beat.

100

Maybe I wouldn't need to use the rope. The worst was behind me and gone forever, I thought. The alcohol was finished and I suddenly had the sobering thought that I'm going to kill myself soon when the sun goes down. I was so drunk by then that I didn't even see or hear a single animal.

'I found a quiet spot on the railway line, far from the road, where I started to shred all the identification documents I had on me. As I was tearing these up I thought of the millions of people who would have paid thousands of rands to get hold of these much-needed documents. The rage, anger and alcohol started to make my head want to explode. Before looking for the perfect tree to hang myself I decided it would be even easier to simply lay down on the railway track and wait to be crushed into a million pieces by a train. To my dismay I suddenly realised it was a Sunday and there were probably no trains that day,' he explains, a small smile flickering across his features at the memory of what he calls 'failure number one'.

'I started moving quicker now, as I could feel the alcohol wearing off. I found a tree and climbed up with the rope around my neck before attaching it to what I thought was a sturdy branch. But as I was letting myself down onto the branch, down to my grave, the rope came loose. Failure number two.

'I walked for another 50 metres and found another perfect tree. Again, up I went, tying the rope around my now aching and bruised neck. How could I fail to kill myself twice in one night? Looking up, I thought I'd never seen so many beautiful stars in the African sky. I remember thinking God was just showing off his beauty and splendour. It was now me against nature. In all things God works for the good of those who love him.

'In a split second after starting to feel dizzy and disoriented

101

from lack of oxygen to both my brain and lungs, I again felt the rope loosening around my neck. In the awkward position I was in, my right leg got stuck on one of the branches and I couldn't even jump or let myself loose.'

At this point in the story, you can almost imagine this as a one-man stage play where Sipho's audience would be sitting spellbound, waiting to hear what comes next. Can this story get any more improbable?

'In one night I'd failed for the third time to commit suicide, so now my new purpose was to survive in a game reserve swarming with wild animals. My head was pounding and my neck was extremely sore from the two failed throttlings. I'd read stories of people saying that as you die you see a white tunnel and white light as your life flashes in front of you. I was too angry and drunk to notice any of that. I just remember gasping for air, which felt like forever. To me, that night, 19 July 2011, God saved me in a sheer miracle.

'My night, though, wasn't over. I cut myself loose from the rope and the tree, and as it was almost midnight and I had no real clue where I was, I ended up walking around in circles in the game reserve until daybreak on the Monday. Then I saw a road construction sign I'd seen the day before, written in Swati, telling me I was in Matiti in Swaziland, not far from the border post. I knew straight away I was in big trouble ...'

In addition to having a sore, bruised neck and ego, Sipho had twisted his ankle and hurt himself falling out of the tree, but these problems paled in comparison to a much larger one. How was he going to cross back into South Africa through the same border post as yesterday, filthy dirty, stinking of cheap booze and with no passport or ID?

'As I neared the border post I plucked up enough courage

to approach a policeman on the Swaziland side. I quickly explained that when I passed through the border yesterday I was robbed of my bag and documents and had to run for my life as thugs were firing at me. That's how I explained my presence in the game reserve and now at the border post.

'He seemed to believe me and led me to the South African Police Station, where he explained my problem to a female officer, who appeared to be very competent and experienced. She asked me questions and then excused herself, going back to her office. In half an hour she returned holding some documents in her hand. With a very serious look on her face she asked me to tell my story again. My second version was totally different from my first. Perhaps I thought it needed to be more believable. She stood up and gently said, "Mr Simelane, I know what happened but I'm going to give you one more chance to tell me the truth."'

Sipho had been busted. 'I knew now I was in real trouble. She knew exactly when I'd crossed the border yesterday and that there was no mugging on either side at that time. She then asked me for my wife's contact details as I'd told her I was married. I left out the part of how I had disappeared from home, "running away" four days ago.'

After another two hours of interrogation by the SAPS and being searched by a male policeman, who was keeping a 'watchful' eye on him, they decided to take Sipho back to the 'crime scene'. The two police officers found it hard to believe that he'd spent a whole night in a game reserve with wild animals around every corner.

'The joke was that not even a mosquito had bitten me – which I think was God talking to me in this malaria-ridden area.

'When we returned once more to the police station, the

female officer disappeared into another room where she called my wife. She came out and asked if I wanted to speak to my wife. When I heard my wife's voice I couldn't hold back the tears. The only words she said was that we'll get through this together and she asked me to pray. Right then I couldn't even remember Psalm 23, the most known and recited verse in the Bible.

'At the crime scene by the railway line, inside the game reserve, the two police officers had picked up a million pieces of shredded identity document, driver's licence, passport and my medical-aid card. Twelve hours later my younger brother Vusi and my father arrived at the police station to take me home.

'I was in a lot of pain and slept the entire seven hours it took to reach home. The following morning I was admitted to a psychiatric clinic where I was reliably informed by the medical staff that for the first three days I couldn't wash myself, feed myself or even take myself to the bathroom.'

For the next 25 days, while Sipho was in the clinic, he tried hard to recall as much detail as possible about what he'd gone through by journalling his thoughts and feelings about anxiety, stress and depression through his verse and prose.

As he moves on to this next part of the story, I hear a different tone in his voice and see a different look on his face. This is obviously where his life story changed. 'The one thing that helped almost more than the medical treatment was being surrounded by other people who'd gone through similar things to me. People I could talk to who understood, and would describe their experiences, always saying that they just wanted to "sleep and not wake up".

'The first days in the clinic were all about sleep, with drugs

104

playing their role here. I was also under suicide watch, although I'm not sure for how long. It's all a bit of a blur now, looking back. The psychiatrist and psychologist were there for me to talk to, explain my feelings to without being judged. Luckily for me, my medical aid allowed for a good clinic with a really pleasant environment.

'With group therapy and my own consultations I was able for the first time to express my feelings in a safe space. It was really freeing. My ideas, emotions and voices might have been there for a long time but only after engaging with the psychologist did I find myself being able to pour everything out in the form of poetry and telling my story. These words were never meant to be published. It was my therapy and at the time I only printed one copy, which was for me.'

Although Sipho may not have realised the importance of this at the time, journalling or writing your thoughts down in the form of prose or poetry is invaluable as therapy.

The natural thing when people hear about others taking their own lives is to question what terrible problems they had. Were they in trouble financially? Were their relationships in trouble? When Robin Williams died through suicide, the world was in a state of collective disbelief – how could someone so funny, so wealthy, so loved, take his own life?

Sipho explains how shocked people were when they heard about his suicide attempt. 'They said, "But he's so successful. He's doing so well in business." Suicide in the black community is a huge thing. There's a massive stigma attached to dying in this way. Depression, stress, anxiety – mental health is generally seen as evil spirits entering the body and is something to be ashamed of and to hide from the community. So when someone takes their own life this is often disguised as something else.

105

"He died of a heart attack." "He was very ill." "She had a long illness." It was never suicide!

'On 7 August 2012, almost one year after my failed suicide attempt, I received a call that something had happened to my father at home. He was 73 years old. All I could hear was a familiar voice on the other end of the phone saying they found my father hanging in our kitchen and he was no more. Unlike me, his son, he never got a second chance.

'We were in a total state of shock, as there were absolutely no signs to point out that he was unhappy in any way. There wasn't a day when he didn't wake up eager to get to work in his tuckshop attached to his house. He'd always been a trader and entrepreneur. He lived with my younger brother who was away working at the time, so he probably saw that as the perfect timing.

'Although we'd never discussed my suicide attempt, I'm pretty sure he knew about it. He'd made up his mind but sadly didn't even leave a letter or note. He just went. My siblings and I decided to tell the truth about what happened because we didn't want to live with the guilt and shame that I'd gone through.'

When someone in the black community dies, the family and community normally come together and hold a night vigil before the burial, with the open casket in the house for people to visit and pay their respects. This, however, is reserved for what the church calls 'the righteous', and not for those who have committed suicide, which is considered the biggest sin.

I see anger in Sipho's eyes as he continues his story. 'For my father this meant no night vigil and on the day of the burial the hearse simply parked outside in the road. The casket was closed to ensure no spirits were released and the body was simply taken to the graveyard and buried. I accepted this at the time but now with the research and writing I've done, together with speaking engagements, meeting academics, theologians and healers, I realise we need to speak openly about these things. We need to educate and be educated.

'In my family alone we have a number of pastors, including my brother and his wife, cousins and an uncle. Did they learn from this? It's hard to say. I know it's going to take a long time for people's views to change because although there's a lot of knowledge out there, there's also deep-seated belief, firmly rooted in the subconscious. They would say, yes, we know a person can be depressed but we can't speak about it. The church when approached by people with mental health issues will advise the person to pray or to seek help ridding them of bad spirits. This, instead of getting real help or medication for their condition.

'I get really frustrated and annoyed at this and want to do all I can to help break down these beliefs and systems. When I posted my experiences on Facebook I was surprised to find about 8 000 people shared my story and more than 14 000 made comments and shared their stories about their spouses, family and friends.

'What people also don't understand is that this isn't some-thing that affects any one group of people. It can happen to you whether you're rich or poor, black, brown or white, young or old. Mental health knows no boundaries.

'Nine years on, I'm now in a good place. With help from mental health professionals my view on life has totally changed and I know they're out there if I need them. I have a lot of self-help and a great support system. Mental health is like being an alcoholic – it's a lifetime thing. Anything could possibly be a trigger and take me back.'

This may be hard to believe, as your overriding image of Sipho is of a man with every confidence in the world.

'I've done a lot of reading and talking to people. I've learnt to accept things I can't change and that it's all right for things to go wrong. I was that guy who always wanted to be in control of how the weather was going to be. It can't rain today. My kids had to get a certain grade. Now I just let it all go. I've made small changes, which add up to me being able to say each day, I'm feeling good. I'm complete. I don't need a new shirt or new sneakers to feel better. I don't need to drive the same cars as the other upwardly mobile parents at my kids' school. I still work to reach goals but now accept that I'll have disappointments along the way.

'My sons know my story and we talk openly about mental health and I think I've impacted the way they think. My youngest son, who is 14, will tell his friends, if he thinks they or their family need help, to talk to me. He knows talking to someone is really important,' he says proudly.

'Perhaps today the biggest change is the speed with which I live my life. I make time to enjoy small things. I've discovered I have green fingers and will take the seeds of a chilli and lovingly plant each one and watch them grow, until I can transplant them into seedlings. When I harvest them it's an appreciation of life and I say, "Wow, I could have missed all of this."

'It's tragic to go through this and not find someone to help you. I've been particularly touched by the elderly people I've spoken to who have some real concerns with their lives. Add to this academics, corporate heads and businesspeople who tell me that if their company knew of their situation they'd lose their jobs. The sad part is, if they went to their bosses and said

108

they'd broken a limb, they'd find sympathy – and time off to recover. When they say they're having mental issues they're viewed as unstable!

'I'm speaking out and I'll keep speaking out. Trying to change hearts and minds.'

A KILLER IN MY HEAD

When I nearly died, it made me sit up and think – hang
    on for a second!
This thing can happen again, any second, minute, hour
    or day,
No one knows the hour or day.

I must wake up and smell the coffee, hurry as quickly
    as I can and do what I like the most, with all those
    dearest to my heart, at my best, soonest moment
    available. Now!
I started to live like I have never lived before.
I could smell all the great aromas and roses I was not
    able to before.
I could now stop and take a deep breath and start
    walking again, appreciating the breathing process
    and its importance.

When the fear of death is long gone, then nothing can
    bother you.
Your sense of who you are will determine your actions
    and what you end up getting in life.
If you see your reach as limited, that you are mostly

109

helpless in the face of so many difficulties, that it's best to keep your ambitions low, then you'll receive the little you expect …

No force or person in this world can stop you from being all you can be.

– Sipho Simelane, 2011

TOOLBOX TIPS

Avoidance doesn't work: try acceptance

❏ It's easy to think that drinking, drugs or going to sleep and not having to wake up is the answer to your problems, but this isn't true.

❏ You can't just take bad feelings away. But you learn to deal with them and carry on. Try to accept what you're feeling.

Accept what you can't control

❏ No one can be happy all the time. It's easy to become overwhelmed when focusing on what you can't control.

❏ Instead, acknowledge what you're feeling and focus on what you *can* do to manage things. Get help if you need it.

❏ Focus on doing what you love, what brings value to your life. Enjoy the small things.

Let it out

❏ If there is no one you can speak to, try writing in a journal – when thoughts and feelings leave the chaos of your mind it's easier to gain perspective about them.

❏ Dancing, singing, drawing, painting, writing poetry and running are all helpful ways to let your feelings out indirectly.

❏ Use mindfulness, self-compassion and affirmations to help you let go.

Educate yourself and others

❏ Learn the signs and symptoms of mental illnesses like depression. It's easier to let go of shame and guilt (often due to stigma) when people understand that what's happening to you isn't your fault.

Suicide shouldn't be a secret

❏ Not speaking about suicide doesn't make the issue go away. Talking about it can save lives.

Mental health versus spiritual or cultural beliefs: find a balance

❏ There's nothing wrong with seeking spiritual or religious help *and* seeking assistance from mental healthcare specialists. Try both.

6

DOBSON DE BEER PROCTER

Depression

Note: Non-binary, or genderqueer, identities are a spectrum of gender identities that are not exclusively masculine or feminine – they are identities outside the 'gender binary'. In Dobson's case, their gender was different from their assigned sex. In Dobson's story, the use of pronouns is therefore gender-neutral – such as when Dobson refers to themself as 'they', 'their' or 'them'.

I first met Dobson a couple of years before doing this interview. My daughter had been at university with their then partner (now wife), Chris, whom our family were very fond of, so we were eager to meet them. I could tell straight away when they told me of their work that Dobson was someone who threw themself into whatever they did with everything they had – including relationships. But it was only when we sat down to do this interview that I discovered the very difficult path they'd had to tread to get where they are today. For Dobson, it hadn't been an easy decision to share this story; I could feel their reluctance, but at the same time their need to help others having similar experiences.

When Dobson de Beer Procter was born in 1987, the family was thrilled to have a second daughter. As usual with a baby girl, there were frilly dresses to be worn and dolls to play with. After all, Dobson's sister loved these things. But once Dobson was able to speak or even show displeasure, it became apparent that what they loved most was running around in shorts – or, even better, with no clothes on – and digging in the mud. 'My parents soon realised that I was a bit of a tomboy, which was no problem for them.

'I suppose I knew from my earliest memories that I was a little different from most girls around me. I certainly wasn't interested in playing with the same things. My parents would buy me dolls, which I wouldn't play with. Dolls, though, sometimes came with a pram, which I found was useful to move stuff around. In fact, one night my parents came to my room to say goodnight and were thrilled to see the pram next to my bed covered with a little blanket. There had to be dolls tucked in – right? Not quite. When they lifted the blanket they came face to face with a collection of frogs, floating around in a pram full of water,' they recall, still laughing at the memory.

'Luckily for me, I had a friend nearby who was also a bit of a tomboy and somehow that normalised things for a while. She would occasionally wear dresses and the bonus was that she had an older brother, who we also got to play with.

'Right from early childhood I was also largely influenced by my parents and their belief systems. My mom is Afrikaans and grew up poor in a small, very conservative Free State town. My father, on the other hand, came from a wealthy English family and had grown up completely differently, with far more privilege. They were married in 1985 and I arrived two years later.

'In 1990 they moved to Butterworth in the Transkei for my father's work, where they lived for around four years. This was when religion took hold of their lives in a big way. They joined a charismatic church movement which originated in Toronto, Canada, which was spreading worldwide.

'This was one of those churches where people practise what they describe as "religious ecstasy, prophesying over people and healing people's emotional wounds". Even though I was very small I remember people singing, shouting and falling over, while speaking in voices that didn't make sense at all. This church had a massive impact on our entire family which lasted for many years.'

I can already tell by Dobson's tone and expression that this church was not a good memory for them.

'Even though I was very shy I was likeable, and a good conversation starter when I was little was always my enormous bush of hair. Everyone else seemed to have "normal" straight hair and there was me with this gigantic head of curls. My earliest memories are happy ones, of running around in my garden in nothing but a pair of red panties with my wild hair flowing out – a little like Mowgli from *The Jungle Book*.

'Primary school was difficult, but mostly because we moved almost every two years. So, just when I'd start making friends I'd be thrust into a new environment – always being the new kid. My mom would continually tell me that God had big plans for me and that I was going to be special.

'While I was still small, being a tomboy wasn't a problem for my mom, but once I was nearing my teens I was told I had to grow up and act in what she considered a proper manner. Tomboyish – or, in my case, "queer" – behaviour stayed in your early childhood and, in my mother's eyes, especially given her background, there was a firm line between masculine and feminine – nothing in between. That was her idea, not mine,

114

and gradually our relationship fell apart.'

Those formative years are often difficult for mother and daughter, but I can tell that for Dobson they were far more than that.

'In 1994, at the age of seven, just before South Africa's first democratic elections, we moved to Knysna. My parents put everything they had into a business that, sadly, failed. Then my dad found a job with a South African company in Nairobi, Kenya, so off we went again. This time I was enrolled in the American International School, where there was no uniform. Heaven for me, as I could go to school in jeans, T-shirts and sneakers, standard skateboarder style, instead of a school uniform dress. Right then, when I wasn't sure where I fitted in, this was perfect.

'Although girls my age also wore pants and T-shirts, the styles were distinctly different, which my mom pointed out to me one day as she was dropping me off. She said, "You should really start dressing differently because everyone's going to think you're a lesbian!" I knew the word but I was shocked. I'd never thought about it. I'd never actually put a name to it or tried to figure out what it was that made me different. As far as I was concerned, I just liked dressing like that. I was confused because we were all pre-teens and I always felt I was observing, not involved in, these scenarios everyone was talking about. For me clothes weren't an issue – they were just comfortable, and after all my mom had bought them for me.

'The lingering effect of her words was an acute feeling of being very ashamed, coupled with homophobia and transphobia that was and is still entrenched in society, which made it worse. I was just 11, a very sensitive age when I was just starting to become more aware of my own gender identity, even though I wasn't able to fully understand it. I'd been given a word – lesbian – which I associated with being bad, so I felt ashamed. Suddenly I became incredibly unhappy and my first bouts with depression kicked in.'

Parents get offended and defensive if other people call their children names. Often, they don't realise how devastating their children's hearing those words from their parents can be, and the long-lasting effect that they can have. At the time, transgender issues were never discussed, and girls and boys were expected to fit into distinct moulds. Today, acceptance of gender issues is slowly increasing – but growing up not quite sure where you fit in is never easy.

'From here my dad was transferred to Tanzania and again I was the new kid on the block – an outsider. Maybe because I was bored with it or just rebelling, I cut my hair really short and in the latest 90s style, as spiky as possible. The problem was this was more of a trend with boys than girls, which I found out the hard way. There was a boy I'd never even met in another grade with the same haircut and somehow we were dubbed the spiky couple. This didn't worry me but it seemed there was a girl who obviously liked him, and to get revenge on me decided to spread the word that the reason I arrived halfway through the term was that I'd got kicked out of Kenya due to the sex work I'd been doing! This led to a massive amount of teasing and bullying to the point where I figured it was easier to say, "It's true," than deny it. I even embellished the story by explaining I charged different amounts of money for different acts. This added fuel to the fire and saw me, at around 13 years old, trying to understand my own identity and sexuality.

'At this point, after another move [to Dar es Salaam] and another school, the depression really kicked in. I remember

116

waking up way before my parents to get ready for school and walking out of my air-conditioned bedroom to be suffocated by the oppressive heat and humidity in the passage, thinking how uncomfortable it was to be alive, in my skin, in this foreign country.'

This was the first time Dobson woke with thoughts of suicide, but felt that it was something you don't talk about. They thought no one would possibly understand, as they had everything they wanted materially so there was nothing to be sad about. 'I thought people only had these thoughts if they had a bad life, and although I didn't like where I was living, that surely wasn't enough to have these thoughts.

'My father's next contract looked like it was going to be in China, where my parents informed me they would send me on ahead so I didn't miss out on any of the school term. This was where I put my foot down and said no chance. At this point in our lives my parents' marriage had been on rocky ground for quite some time, with divorce papers coming and going many times. My mom was still fanatically religious but my dad now gave it a miss. All of this added to my firm decision that I needed to go to boarding school, in South Africa not China.'

The decision was made to send Dobson to an all-girls boarding school in Pretoria where, for the first time since telling their parents about their unhappiness, they were seen by a school counsellor. After a couple of sessions the counsellor recommended professional help. With Dobson's parents' approval, it was decided that Dobson would see a psychologist contracted to the school.

'A part of me felt the school counsellor couldn't wait to pass me on to someone else, as she was uncomfortable discussing issues of gender and sexuality. The school, being Anglican, was very conservative, as was the staff – especially when I was used to the American International School. It turned out she did me a favour, as for the first time after seeing the psychologist I started to feel listened to.'

The era of the child being seen and not heard may be over, but the importance of listening to children should never be underestimated. For Dobson, this was a step forward.

'This was my third school in the last year and three different educational systems and assessments, seeing me taken from Grade 7 to Grade 10 at the age of 14. Although I'd always done really well academically, I realised when I reached boarding school that I'd missed out on basic foundational maths and science. I'd always enjoyed maths but suddenly being thrown into Grade 10 maths left me floundering and my marks dropping. My other subjects were fine, but as I'd had my heart set on becoming a vet this was a serious setback.'

Knowing how clever Dobson is and how hard they work to achieve academically, I could understand their frustration.

'By the end of my first term in 2002, my therapist said she was going to have a meeting with my mom to give her feedback on our sessions. This was a shock as I couldn't imagine the therapist sharing what I'd told her – that I knew I was gay. She, on the other hand, felt it was in my mom's best interests. I explained that when she met my mom she'd really like her and find her charming, but that I really didn't think giving her this information was a good idea.

'Of course she ended up telling my mom something along the lines of Dobson's been going around telling friends she's gay.' At this point, Dobson was still seen as a girl, even though they weren't. 'After this session, being the end of term I went to fetch my bags before meeting my mom in the car park, where

118

my equally religious uncle was waiting to take me to his place with my mom for the weekend. As I walked towards her I saw her burst into tears and my heart sank. She'd been told my news. I said I was really sorry but she refused to listen, saying it's not true and I mustn't talk about it. The drive home was awkward in the extreme.'

With homosexuality being seen as almost criminal, and a mortal sin in the eyes of the church, Dobson felt as though they were guilty of something massive. At a time when they needed support, they were rejected. I wait while they pause before going on; this is hard for them to talk about.

'The next morning my mom and uncle took me to his church where the pastor and his wife formed a circle around me, while they tried to deliver me from the demons who obviously had taken over my mind and body. I was furious and enormously traumatised and ran out of there halfway through their "exorcism". The pastor told my mom it was the demons in my head that made me so angry I ran away.

'After this scenario, the holiday was a nightmare. My mom was torn between being incredibly angry and at the same time scared because she was convinced I was going to hell. Dad seemed almost indifferent. He was away for work most of the time these days and rarely at home.

'Not having my parents' acceptance made my depression worse as I now found I couldn't even go to them with mundane, everyday issues like fighting with someone at school, because there was this "other matter" hanging over everything.' Once the trust and link between a parent and child is gone, it's a long road to regain it.

'Finally, after being in so many schools and battling to make friends, boarding school saw me actually making some great friends. Amongst them was one special girl who became my first girlfriend and whose family quickly became like my own. She was a weekly boarder so I spent most weekends at her home with her wonderful, accepting family. My mother by then had taken to calling me names and even bought me a book about hell, which was where she reliably informed me I was going. When my girlfriend's mother found out about this she was furious, and called my dad to tell him to step up and protect me. I'm not sure what happened to the book but I never saw it again. My dad, of course, never said a word to me about my mom and her behaviour – a pattern that would be repeated for years to come.' Dobson is unable to hide the frustration in their voice.

'By Grade 11, things were a lot better. I had a great group of friends and found, as I'd openly come out as being gay, that I would receive surreptitious notes, often late at night, from girls asking for my advice. They'd say, *I think I feel like this also but I don't know what to do about it.* That's probably where the idea of becoming a psychologist took root in my mind.

'This wasn't the first time I found myself playing the role of counsellor. My mom knew no boundaries as to child–mother relationships and would confide in me about her marriage – way too much, too often. It was no surprise when my best subject during my psychology studies turned out to be family therapy.

'Sadly, my relationship with my school girlfriend ended when she met a guy. I was devastated, which she couldn't understand, saying she thought I'd be happy for her. Why would I be happy when she traded me for a new partner? It was really difficult as I'd become part of her family – which now meant her boyfriend also. This situation saw my depression

120

come back with a bang. From being really happy to being really sad.'

These situations can be a disaster waiting to happen, as it was in Dobson's case.

'I felt a lot of angst and pain at this breakup, and although I'd been cutting [self-injuring] myself from 13, I'd never done any serious harm to myself. Up to now. Perhaps I thought that dropping hints of what I felt and what I wanted to do would somehow bring my ex-girlfriend back to me but she didn't respond to my hints. Luckily another friend, Abi – still one of my best friends to this day – took me seriously. She was hor-rified when she arrived in my room that night to see what I'd tried to do [cutting my wrists] and stayed awake, watching over me in case I tried again. The next morning she went to the chaplain and spoke to him because she told me it was too much for her to hold. I told her I understood and didn't feel she'd betrayed me.'

Abi had done the right thing. Whether Dobson really wanted to end their life or not, they had given a call for help. When people say that a suicide attempt isn't serious, and that someone was just 'looking for attention', know that for every failed attempt another may succeed. This attention is never unwarranted.

Later that day, Dobson was called to go and see the chaplain, who told them that he'd organised a therapist to see them. 'She was a life coach and really cool with kids, not being fazed by me or my situation. I saw her for a couple of weeks, which was really helpful, and somehow I felt back on track. Something had shifted inside me with the kind of love and support from this woman and shortly after I started dating another girl and felt I was in a really good place.

121

'That was until I got a call from my dad saying he was taking me out of boarding school to move back with him and my mom to Knysna. I was really upset as for the first time in my whole school career I felt I fitted in and had just started a new relationship with another girl. This was a really formative relationship for both of us, and as she was also struggling with depression and self-harming we had real empathy and understanding for one another. Even though our relationship ended at the time she's been an important part of my life and is still supporting me today in my transgender journey.

'To add to it my marks weren't great and to my horror my parents made me repeat Grade 11 back in Knysna. This meant an extra year while all my friends went on to matric. I felt really left behind.'

Dobson went on to have weekly sessions with a Knysna psychologist for the next two years, which were a space for reflection and healing, they explain. Yet no one suggested that Dobson see a psychiatrist or start taking antidepressants. 'I think my mom was really behind this move back to Knysna, as here she felt she'd have more control over me to stop what she saw as my evil lifestyle,' says Dobson, sighing at the memory.

'Sadly my next relationship also broke down and this time my parents were around to see my sadness. One afternoon my dad came to my room and said, "My babes, I just want you to know if you're crying over a boy or girl it doesn't matter. What matters to me is that you're crying." I burst into tears and told him I was crying over a girl. He stood up and said, "I'm really sorry, I can't talk to you about it," and left the room. I felt even more devastated.

'Years later, while my parents were getting divorced, my dad and I did a road trip to Namibia and around a campfire one night I bought that conversation up and asked why he did that. He said he really wanted to be there for me but didn't want to upset my mom. He said things were so tough between them then, she would have instantly divorced him, which wasn't what he wanted then. They fought to keep their marriage alive even though it was a terrible one.'

After matric, Dobson decided to do a BA majoring in psychology. Their mother's continuous brainwashing, though, had left its mark. 'I started to think that perhaps I didn't have to feel the way I did. Maybe I wasn't meant to be queer, and so in my second year at varsity I chose to do conversion therapy.' The Wikipedia description of this says it all: 'The pseudoscientific practice of trying to change an individual's sexual orientation from homosexual or bisexual to heterosexual using psychological or spiritual interventions.'

'It was a six-month programme with weekly meetings, teachings and small prayer therapy groups. My mom, of course, was really happy about this, although it did nothing to heal the now-gaping rift between us. Part of the theory was that you didn't get enough attention and love from your mother – that's why you're into other girls. Absolute bullshit. Throughout the process I was having conversations with my mom about this idea and my feeling was that I was doing it so she would accept me. I now realise I didn't choose to do it to get her approval but rather from my *own* homophobia and huge shame, and not wanting to be like that any more. At boarding school I was out and proud but as soon as I was home I was the complete opposite. It was like leading a dual life, which was why I ended up being so happy at boarding school. I didn't have to act – I could be myself.

'I did the entire conversion course, took a break and repeated it the following year. I did all the right things. I attended church and started dating boys. Then I was in trouble with the conversion therapy people for having sex before marriage. I found it all very complicated, especially when the first serious guy I went out with actually raped me. It certainly wasn't consensual. When my mom found out she was very supportive and immediately put me on birth control. Although, of course, she was totally anti-sex before marriage, it was a lot more acceptable than having a gay child. She felt maybe I was on the right track at last. By now I wasn't seeing a therapist as I was talking to someone at the church.'

While counselling within religion can, in the right circumstances, be beneficial, it can't take the place of professional mental health intervention. Conversion therapies have been exposed as dangerous and discredited countless times, yet they're sadly still around.

'There are always many narratives in people's lives and for me there were multiple, significant narratives that played a role in my depression and suicidality. All the queer confusion and my parents' issues, not to mention sexual abuse in my early childhood.' I look up from my notes at this revelation and can see that this is something Dobson came to terms with, but did not accept, long ago.

Dobson had been sexually abused by different people from the age of four – friends and family friends – and hadn't told their parents until much later. Their mom's reaction? 'Don't worry, what happened to me was worse. You'll be fine.'

'I only discovered later that my mom had really laid into a certain teenage boy who'd been involved. But the fact remained I felt she was dismissive of me and my feelings. In fact, she was fiercely protective and didn't want me to be hurt, but somehow

124

didn't want to acknowledge what was happening.

'When the abuse began I started developing a stutter and would get panic attacks at school. This was just before we'd moved to Kenya and my dad was rarely at home. My life was in turmoil and this naturally would add to my future problems.'

A part of Dobson's life has always been about helping others. Before the conversion therapy began, they started a small NGO called Rape Outcry, which they ran for about seven years. 'We developed poster campaigns on raising awareness around rape and rape culture, and I started a support group with students, doing a lot of research. This fitted right in with my determination to become a psychologist, so I began a BA Psychology which also allowed me to start counselling within this group. I was desperately trying to lead a heterosexual life and run the NGO together with hectic studying and doing research for the varsity's HIV/Aids project – which were all really just a distraction. I wasn't sleeping at all though and was quite manic.' Mania can often be part of depression, and can take over a person's life.

'Shortly after my second conversion therapy I got a scholarship to go to Germany and work on a campaign about sexual abuse for six months. It was a wonderful experience until one day it wasn't. Being on a tight budget in Europe, but wanting to take advantage of the travel opportunities, I worked extra jobs and travelled as much as possible. All this time, I tried to stay in a heterosexual headspace. I couldn't say I was hetero but I wasn't going to be with a woman. I wasn't necessarily looking to get married but at least not engage in any sexual acts. I also worked out celibacy didn't suit me.'

Like many students, Dobson used the CouchSurfing homestay and social networking service to find free accommodation

in the places they visited. 'Everywhere I travelled I told people about Rape Outcry and the Do You See campaign. In each
country, I found people who assisted in translating the posters into their local languages so they could also use them. This
took off especially well in Dublin, as my friend who lived there
helped me make contact with several artists in the city.'

After Dobson left, a gallery hosted a month-long exhibition
of their art and posters raising awareness about sexual abuse in
Ireland – and a similar exhibit by art students where they were
studying. 'I wasn't there to see this exhibition because I flew
back to South Africa earlier than I was supposed to after my
own traumatic experience of being raped in a hotel in Venice.
This really threw me and I knew there was no coming back
from this. All I wanted now was to go home to South Africa.
The next day on a train heading out of Venice I locked myself
in a little bathroom and called my dad. He started asking me
for details about what happened – all the medical stuff. I told
him I knew all about that as I'd worked with it. What I needed
now was emotional support. I felt unsafe and needed to get out
of there – fast. Eventually I flew to friends in Dublin, where I
received so much love and support. They're confirmed atheists
and being with them made me ask some really big existential
questions about religion, question everything I'd been fed for
so many years.'

There are moments when we need to stop just to catch a
collective breath as this moving and dramatic story unfolds.

Returning to South Africa, Dobson managed to do their
psychology internship through Families South Africa (FAMSA)
and Rape Outcry. Even after having their anti-religious
epiphany in Ireland, they started attending church again. 'Then
somehow I found myself engaged – to a man. You'd think my

parents would be ecstatic. They weren't – they hated him. I'd known him from church and thought if I have to be with a man for the rest of my life it might as well be a friend. Someone I get on really well with and enjoy their company. He knew my background and as he came from an incredibly broken one himself it wasn't an issue. The only problem was that he had a real problem with the truth and eventually I realised I couldn't live with this constant lying.

'At the same time I'd met a woman, Elizabeth, at church and we soon became close friends. It wasn't something I rushed into this time. It happened slowly, together with a combination of being disillusioned around my relationship with my fiancé. Now, having travelled, I had a more integrated experience of the world, plus what I'd learnt from my psychology studies to guide me.

'At school, when I realised I was gay I started journalling. I was really disciplined about it and by the time I was at varsity had quite a stash of books. I really feel this saved me and stopped me feeling isolated. I'd read up on techniques for journalling and mine wasn't a gratitude journal but related what was happening to me at that time. I also painted a lot, which was another kind of therapy.'

Journalling is now a firm part of many 'toolboxes' to do with mental health, and a great outlet for feelings and thoughts.

Shortly after breaking off their engagement, Dobson and Elizabeth became partners. They decided to keep their relationship a secret, which they did for the next two and a half years. This was easy: two young women sharing a flat was normal.

'We totally got away with it and I thought all was well until I caught her cheating on me. This was her plan, as she was so worried someone would find out about us she would hook up with guys in public who she knew would talk. She came from a very complex, conservative, Afrikaans community and I knew it was hard for her.

'All this plus what had happened in Italy led me to see my GP for help. I'd been put on an antidepressant previously but had taken myself off it as I didn't like the side effects. My GP then put me on another medication that worked and which I'm still on, which definitely helped at the time. I was also seeing a therapist who helped me with my relationship issues. My partner and I even went to joint sessions.

'But by the end of 2012, I couldn't take this complex relationship any more and decided to go to Cape Town where I enrolled for a master's degree. I told her if she really wanted to give our relationship a chance, there couldn't be any more secrets. A couple of months later she called and said she did want to be with me. She came out to her parents and her mom refused to talk to her. Her mother tried to call me to tell me her daughter's not gay and I was just a bad influence on her.

'By then my parents were getting divorced and I found out my father was already seeing someone else. It took three and half years for them to finally divorce, during which I got message after message from my mom blaming the divorce on me because I was living a life of sin and now he was also. According to her we wanted to be sinful together without having her righteousness. She told me she was removing herself from my life, blocked my number and deleted me off all her social media. That was it – for the next three and a half years I didn't see or talk to her.

'At the end of my internship my relationship had finally run its course and my partner and I split up. We even went for couples therapy to figure out how to break up without losing each other, and today remain good friends.'

Now working and doing community service, Dobson was able to buy a flat and a car, which gave them a great sense of achievement. 'One day I called my mom and said I'm going to be in Knysna and could we meet for coffee. She said she was in tears and had been waiting for this. She flew me down shortly after for my sister's birthday. This was strange as I'd had minimal contact with my very religious, married sister who, with her husband and children, lives with my mom and gran. Four generations under one roof – all very religious.

'Even though on the surface this should have been a good time and I felt I was adulting quite well, somehow the depression kicked in again and with it the suicidal thoughts. I went to another GP who increased my medication, adding an extra one. I also realised I needed and deserved to see a psychiatrist and found a brilliant one who, after reviewing my medication, got me on better meds.'

Having studied psychology, Dobson knew what these suicidal thoughts could lead to. If you don't feel right about your medication, there's no harm in getting a second or even a third opinion, as getting your medication right is crucial to coping.

After finishing community service, Dobson was 'scarily' unemployed for six months and in serious student-loan debt for their postgraduate studies. This led to sleepless nights and much stress. They finally got a post, where they remain today, at a government mental health organisation. 'I started doing psycho-legal work for an NGO, while also doing sessional work until my government post became my full-time job. My luck must have been really changing because this is also when my friend Tai introduced me to my future wife Chris, who I instantly fell in love with. I then went on to introduce Tai to my dear school friend Abi, who today is his wife!

'My work, although going well, was really difficult to deal with in the beginning on an emotional level. Each day I was dealing with cases of extreme abuse, which at the time I found hard to deal with and which once again pulled me down into depression. This was hard because my life on the surface was going so well. I had this woman who I adored and who loved me, my friends who were my family, a promising career, and was now busy with a PhD, which is what I'd always looked forward to. How could I be unhappy? But I ignored it and didn't even talk to Chris about it. I'd go two or three weeks where things would be fine and I was managing and then I'd come home and within half an hour would start crying for no real reason at all.'

Every time Dobson mentions Chris, their features change. I can see the difference Chris made in their life, although there were still tough times ahead. I speak to Chris, and this is what she tells me.

'I knew from day one about Dobson's depression. It was never a secret, especially given their career path. It was always something that was out in the open.

'Funnily enough, with my calm, low-lying type of personality I'm often attracted to people who have real fire in them, which often comes with a bit of pain. Also, a lot of people I've known and loved over the years have had mental health issues and it's never been something that's scared me off. My own sister and several friends have been down this road.

'With Dobson I look at it as something we have to talk about and deal with. At first I had to wrap my head around it and become more acquainted with what I was dealing with, but they're always teaching me about psychology and the different types of mental health. It's an ongoing conversation.'

One day, Dobson had a particularly difficult, painful experience with a client who was unfairly admitted to hospital and who desperately wanted their help to get out. 'As I delved into what appeared to be a dark, cloak-and-dagger type of case, I realised I didn't have the power to change her circumstances, which was hard for her to hear. This added to my depression and when I got home I started crying and couldn't stop. Chris tried to help but didn't really know what to do. I couldn't talk to her. A friend messaged Chris to ask us to go out for drinks with them. I said I couldn't go while I felt like this but that she should go as she didn't need to deal with me like this. Reluctantly she left.'

You may be wondering how Chris could not have realised what Dobson was going through. But think about it – we all have 'bad days' and 'very bad days'. And Dobson was reluctant to talk about what they really felt. Had they talked …

As we move on to the final and most dramatic part of their story, Dobson tenses. 'I knew Chris's doctor had given her some anxiety medication, a sort of sedative, so I grabbed these and a bottle of whisky, plus some of my own meds, seeing this as a way to leave all my pain behind. Had I been sober I would never have taken what would be termed a substance-induced near-suicide so far.

'Just before I did this I messaged Chris to tell her I was fine. I then sent a message to Abi's boyfriend Tai, who said he'd call me later. By the time he called he could hear I was totally out of it and came rushing over, opening the door with spare keys him and Abi had. They sat with me for an hour and a half having this long conversation before I passed out. They were now faced with the issue of whether to take me to hospital, which would cause a lot of drama, or risk keeping me at home and my dying. Looking back and knowing now the effects of what I'd ingested, I should have gone to hospital. Once again it was Abi who, 15 years after my first suicide attempt, stayed up with me in the same situation again.

'By the time Chris came home, a little worse for wear from a night's drinking, Tai and Abi told her that I'd gone to sleep but that she needed to be here with me. They didn't want to say too much as they were worried she wouldn't be able to process and deal with it right then. Naturally, the next day it all came out and it's still something Chris and I find difficult to talk about as she feels guilty for having left me.' There is raw emotion in Dobson's voice.

'The day after this was horrible,' recalls Chris. 'I knew I just had to get through the day and it took around a month before I started to feel a bit better. We did a lot of talking and naturally I had to work through my own guilt – of going out that night and leaving Dobson alone. We were lucky enough to find an incredible therapist who we've seen together and who's made a big difference to our lives. Before we got married we also went to couples therapy. This helped us work through a lot of really tough things, not just about that night but about how to partner someone suffering from depression. How to talk about it, and be more sensitive to their needs and to just be there to listen when they need you.

'I do find myself looking for signs when Dobson's had a particularly bad day or if I go somewhere alone. It's always at the back of my mind. They made me a promise to never leave me and I believe that.

'In the beginning I was advised to hold and dispense their meds each day, which at the beginning I did. This felt like I was helping by taking at least that responsibility onto my shoulders. It gave me some power, which helped then.'

Dobson was immediately booked off for a month by their psychiatrist, with their boss and close colleague's backing, after hearing what happened.

'Before my near-suicide I'd stupidly cut down on some of my medications, which I realised after was a big mistake, so the psychiatrist quickly sorted this out and to this day there's no way I'd ever change my meds again.

'My life now couldn't be better. Chris and I got married at the end of 2018 and although my mother couldn't bring herself to be there, our relationship is slowly coming right. My dad and sister came to the wedding and although I know this wasn't easy for my sister, in particular, they were there for me. My dad loves Chris and immediately accepted our relationship.' The happiness radiates from them thinking about this.

'Chris's mom and I have a wonderful relationship. I was the first woman Chris ever introduced to her mother and we got on really well from day one. Even though she's gone through her own, quite painful, journey with Chris when she first came out, everything is really good there now.'

'Now life is good and Dobson is definitely on the right track, handling the workload in a sensible way,' Chris tells me. 'There are certain things that come up at work that they now understand can't always be solved.

'Depression can be incredibly personal and also really lonely and it's hard to take full control of someone's mental health yourself. Having your tribe, a community around you, makes a massive difference. Other people you can talk to and share your partner's journey, especially through difficult times, means not having to deal with everything on your own. I need to take care of my own mental health to be strong enough for Dobson.

'Getting therapy has been key to going forward, although there were times when we'd walk out of a therapy session thinking wow, will we make it? How could this be even more difficult? It can be a painful, growing experience, but an essential one. If you can get through this with your partner you'll see each other grow and edge closer into yourselves,' says Chris assuredly.

And what of Dobson's dreams today? 'I work with particularly vulnerable people in terms of mental illness. Both my work and research involves trans, suicide and people with disabilities, as well as continuing with the trauma work, psycho-legal and Eye Movement Desensitisation and Reprocessing (EMDR) – a psychotherapy treatment originally designed to alleviate the distress associated with traumatic memories.

'I'm still busy with my PhD but I'm in a really good space. We spent Christmas with my family and are now included in family occasions. It's what you'd call a work in progress.

'My PhD is on suicide and through my research I've learnt it's not just the mental illness side but also the contextual side that's equally important. My research is centred on looking at cases of trans and gender-diverse people [people who have a gender identity or expression that differs from their sex assigned at birth]. I look at their life experiences and their depression, and dysphoria which is linked to depression. Dysphoria centres around embodied experiences which impact a person's internal and external worlds, their relationship with themselves and others. They feel their external world doesn't affirm their internal one, living in a transphobic and cisnormative world.

'For me in particular, it's all about the identity struggle to be accepted as a non-binary person. In other words, I was assigned female at birth but I don't identify within the binary as a woman or man and I do struggle with dysphoria but in different ways than before. My pronouns are they/them – a gender-neutral pronoun used for a singular person, usual who is non-binary but not necessarily. "They" was even Merriam-Webster's 2019 word of the year because of its growing popularity. Similarly, instead of using Ms or Mr, my title is Mx [soon to be replaced by Dr!].'

Dobson is infinitely patient with me as I make notes trying to take all this new information in. I appreciate the importance of this to Dobson and want to make sure I don't slip up in the retelling of their story.

'It's so freeing and affirming to have language evolve and words which resonate with my experience. I'm still trying to work through this, and with my research and work I'm becoming a specialist in this field. Having your identity affirmed or being acknowledged as you grow up – this is the story of my life.

'Trans people can be non-binary like me, or genderqueer, agender, or fit more within the binary, in other words, assigned female at birth when they're a man, and usually but not always going through some form of a gender-confirming transition to have their gender align with their true identity or the other way around. It can be very confusing for friends and family at first but it's the effort that counts and you'll eventually get used to it if you continue to try,' they assure me.

'I know now that suicide could never again be an option for me because of the damage it causes the survivors. But saying that, I also know the pain and agony you personally go through and that it's not about other people. It's a very complex situation. During my speech at our wedding I made certain promises to Chris. Not many people there understood the real meaning when I said that above all I would stay, and I must hold myself to that.'

TOOLBOX TIPS

Let go of gender roles
- ❏ Gender has been understood in a binary way ('girl' or 'boy') for centuries, yet it's more complex. Gender is fluid, with people's gender existing more on a spectrum.
- ❏ Characteristics (for example, being strong/ independent/caring/sensitive) and interests (for example, liking pink/blue/playing sports/cooking) are assigned to specific gender roles, which should be a thing of the past.

A child is an independent human, not an extension of a parent
- ❏ Children have their own thoughts, beliefs and desires. These aren't passed down genetically – they're personal.
- ❏ Don't force your dreams onto your child. This pressure can result in a host of mental health problems.
- ❏ Parents know their children better than anyone, but shouldn't make assumptions about who they are or

136

what their lives will be like in the future. If parents' expectations aren't met, the relationship will suffer.

Your prejudices don't go unheard or unfelt

❑ Be aware of your commentary around your children. They pick up more than you think.

❑ Expressing racism, homophobia, transphobia, misogyny, fat shaming and so on may not seem harmful, but your child will internalise the message that it's bad to fall within these categories.

Children need safe spaces to express how they feel

❑ Children need to know it's okay to not be okay, even if they don't have a reason why.

❑ They're learning how to process difficult feelings, and require guidance and support. Therapy can help if it's difficult for them to open up to their parents.

Religion is a belief; being gay or transgendered is an identity

❑ People choose what they believe in, whereas they don't necessarily choose who they're naturally attracted to or how they feel most comfortable in their own bodies.

❑ No amount of praying will change someone's sexual or gender identity. Believing that it will can cause significant difficulties with self-acceptance and mental health in general.

Learn to manage marriage issues

❑ Sending a child to therapy to 'get fixed' when parents

themselves can't manage their own problems can damage a child.

Going into 'fix it' mode isn't always helpful

❑ When children are in pain, they need you to listen and support them without judgement. Trying to fix things is just a way for you to feel in control, and isn't necessarily helpful to them.

❑ If you can't tolerate difficult emotions, go to therapy. It's not your child's job to make sure you don't have uncomfortable feelings. They need you to be there when they have difficult feelings.

Progress in mental health is not linear

❑ Depression is episodic: things can go well for however long, then you can return to a depressive state again. This is hard to accept – but remember, it's not your fault. That's just how depression works.

Language matters

❑ The words we use to describe people can be the difference between whether people feel that they belong or don't belong. Language plays a significant role in everyday life.

❑ Instead of avoiding getting it wrong, ask for clarification. If you show you're trying, it's okay to make a mistake. Be open to learning something new – a small amount of effort can make a significant difference to someone else.

7

ALEXANDRA WALLIS

Postnatal depression

For nine months, everyone tells you how wonderful it will be when you have your baby, especially when you've been trying to start a family for a while. This is everything you've ever dreamed of – right?

This certainly wasn't the case for Alexandra Wallis when at the age of 30 in 2011 she gave birth to her much-awaited son Anthony and experienced her own hell – postnatal depression (PND).

With Alex, as she likes to be called, in KwaZulu-Natal and me in Johannesburg, we do the interview via Skype. Although we're a screen apart, it feels almost as good as sitting together over coffee. Having looked up her Mums Support Network online, I know she has a large following, which is growing daily – one of the few such resources for moms, especially in her province. I'm eager to learn more about her and how she turned her postpartum depression into such a force for good. Hearing her slightly British accent, I begin by asking where she came from originally.

'I'd moved here with my family from England when I was 16. Although my husband Paul is Durban born and bred, I didn't have any family or friends here who were having babies at the time, so I had no experience of what I should expect from pregnancy or childbirth. I also didn't realise that having a Type A personality, along with being a control freak, would make the whole experience a lot harder. To say I like things organised is a bit of an understatement. Super-organised is what I really want, which is my way of dealing with anxiety. Now I know these are all huge risk factors for postnatal depression.

'Before I fell pregnant, I was working as a physiotherapist, and although I'd suffered from anxiety my whole life, I'd been told growing up that I was just a shy, nervous child. Once I'd been diagnosed with PND so many aspects of my life clicked into place. I remember waking up for school not being able to have breakfast and feeling nauseous. When I was at university I'd been treated for mild depression a couple of times, but didn't think anything of this when I was pregnant. Not once during the whole nine months did anyone ask about my mental health. You're handed a leaflet saying this is SADAG and if you're struggling call them. In my mind PND was just lying in bed all day crying – so I thought I would be able to spot that quite easily. And then there's the fact that no one talks about what it's really like for fear of the stigma attached.'

This is quite amazing when statistics show that up to 40 per cent of new mothers may develop PND, which can have long-lasting effects, not just on the mother but on the baby and the whole family. Even baby and parenting magazines give PND very little coverage. If new moms were more aware of what to expect, even if it doesn't happen to them, stories like Alex's would be very different.

Alex initially struggled to fall pregnant, which at the time seemed like a goal she had to achieve. She didn't think past that step. As her pregnancy progressed, so did her anxiety, although she didn't realise it. 'I thought this probably wasn't how I should be feeling but I didn't want to admit it. People always say, "I bet you can't wait to meet the baby," "I bet you're so thrilled, so happy" – and I wasn't, but how could I say this? My expected reaction would have been how thrilled and excited I was – but I wasn't. When the wife of one of my husband's colleagues said to me she was sick of being pregnant and couldn't wait to meet her baby, I remember thinking, *I'm the opposite. I don't want this baby ever to come out* but I couldn't say it – to anyone.

'What I didn't know was that this was the beginning of PND. I just thought every mother-to-be felt like this – doesn't everyone get a bit nervous before having a baby? I had no idea what was about to hit me. What I also didn't know was that many women have prenatal depression and/or anxiety and that in fact they now use the term perinatal distress, which covers any time in the perinatal [immediately before and after the birth] period. The definition includes feelings of compulsion, anxiety, depression and rage, amongst other symptoms, but it's really hard to admit these feelings.

'Being a control-freak Type A, of course I had my birth plan. I wanted a natural birth with no medication involved, which is what I got, but it wasn't the happy, exciting day I was expecting. My labour progressed very quickly. At first I was having what I thought were my usual daily Braxton Hicks contractions – but it turned out I have an irritable uterus, so I didn't even realise I was in labour for the first few hours.

'Anthony was originally due on the 11th of January but eventually came on the 20th. We'd been on tenterhooks for weeks as in mid-December we were told he'd fully descended into the birth canal and his head was engaged, ready for birth.

For weeks the feeling of dread and unease had been build-ing, when suddenly labour kicked in really quickly, with me doubled over in pain and blood everywhere. I was rushed to the hospital and even though I was asking for something for the pain (I didn't realise I was in the final stages of labour and thought I would be feeling this intensity for hours) there was no time. The baby was also a posterior presentation, meaning he was facing the wrong way, which made things even more painful. Within an hour of arriving at the hospital he was born and relief washed over me. Not happiness or love for my child, just relief that the pain was over.'

Once again, television and the movies have a lot to answer for. Those perfect newborn babies cradled lovingly in their mothers' arms just moments after the birth, a loving father looking on, don't always happen – and you immediately feel you've failed.

'I'd had no interventions or medications, which was how I'd wanted it, but it was really tense and scary, especially as his heart rate kept dropping during the delivery and everyone seemed quite frantic. He was born at 6:35 in the evening and after everything had been cleared up and he'd been weighed, suddenly it was shift change for the nursing staff. This meant they had to move me out of the labour ward and into a mater-nity ward with no time in between to rest and recover, or lie with the baby. Everything was happening so fast. They were also trying to find me some food as I hadn't eaten since lunch-time and soon after that it was 9 pm. They made Paul and my doula [birth support professional] leave for the night. Even though the doula didn't manage to do much, given the speed of the birth, it would have been good to have her and Paul around a little longer for support.

142

'Then it was bedtime and I'd decided to have Anthony room in with me – which wasn't the best idea, with hindsight. I was exhausted from the birth and in a huge amount of pain, along with trying to process what had happened. Now I was left all on my own with this baby and I had no idea what to do. I don't think I slept that night because he just screamed and screamed. I was struggling to breastfeed and felt hopeless as I didn't really know what to do but was too embarrassed to call a nurse. I am his mother; I should be able to do this – right? What's the matter with me?'

Alex weighs in on the notion that every woman can breastfeed. 'If ever there was a myth, this was it. I had this idea that instinctively I'd know how to do it but being the shy, polite person I am, I thought, *It's the middle of the night, I shouldn't bother the staff*, so I just pushed through. It's hard to imagine but even with the baby screaming his lungs out no one came in to help me. The next day when the gynaecologist and the paediatrician arrived, they could see I was in tears and totally overwhelmed, but they completely ignored this and did the required check on me and Anthony and promptly left. Today I hear this same story from new moms, that healthcare professionals rarely ask about your mental health – they just ignore it.'

I remember many nights when my own now-grown son was a baby, waking every hour for a feed. It was both scary and exhausting, with the strangest thoughts going through your head – thoughts not easily shared, for fear of being judged.

One thing you're never short of before you have a baby is advice from anyone and everyone – whether you want it or not. 'I'd been insistent on going home the day after the birth as I'd been told I should leave the hospital as soon as possible if I wanted to breastfeed the baby exclusively, as otherwise the staff might try to give the baby a bottle. So I discharged myself and went home. What was I thinking? I had no help at home – only someone to clean once a week – and Paul, anticipating the birth in December, had already taken too much leave. I'd given birth on the Thursday, went home on the Friday and Paul went back to work on the Monday.'

All this time, no one thought to look at Alex's mental health. How was she coping? Did she need help?

Many mothers will sympathise with Alex as she continues. 'So here I was, all alone in the house with this baby and no idea what to do. I was also in a lot of pain from the episiotomy [surgical cut to aid difficult delivery], added to which I discovered Anthony was what is known as a high-needs baby, meaning he wanted to be on me (and *only* me) all the time, which didn't include sitting down, so I'd just walk around with him attached to me like a piece of clothing – otherwise he would scream. Durban at the end of January is also boiling hot and humid, and we didn't have air conditioning, which all added to my discomfort and utter exhaustion. I felt on edge and jittery, but I still didn't know this was anxiety. Somehow I thought this was normal and that every new mother went through this, which led to the question – why was this so hard for me? Why couldn't I deal with it? I came to the conclusion I was just a terrible mother if I couldn't take all this in my stride. It was all I'd ever wanted my whole life – not to be a careerwoman but to be a mother – and now I hated it.'

I can see on her face and hear in her voice the pain she still feels at these memories, which have spurred her on in her quest to stop other mothers feeling this way.

'I remember when we would visit family and people would try to take him from me for a while so that I could eat or get

144

some rest, but he was inconsolable out of my arms and that made people feel uncomfortable. They would quickly hand him back to me so I never managed to get a break.

'After continually walking up and down with Anthony attached to me, I'd try and put him down in his cot so I could have just a little time to myself but five minutes later I'd hear a cry – my body would react with a stab of terror. This saw my anxiety going through the roof but all the time I kept everything to myself as I was too embarrassed to tell anyone that I wasn't coping, and that I didn't feel the special bond, which surely every mother had, with my baby. Everyone says you're going to fall in love instantly and I believed that, so when it didn't happen, once again it had to be my fault. Instead of falling in love with him I was terrified and resentful of him.'

These days, Alex knows it's quite normal not to feel that instant bond: it's a new relationship and sometimes it can take a little time to get to know each other. 'It's just as normal as falling in love with your partner. With my second child, Olivia, three years later, I felt that instant bond – but with Anthony I just thought I must be a terrible mother. I truly believed he didn't like me and he might be better off without me, as it seemed to me that I couldn't satisfy his needs. How I was struggling, the exhaustion, terror – the feelings that I thought were abnormal – were actually normal and common, and what I thought was my failing as a mother was actually PND. Women are very good at just pushing on and getting through the hard times. I did try to talk to people but they would say, "It's hard for everyone and you're doing fine – just keep going, it will be okay." No one really connected and said, "Let's help you out."'

Hearing this, I also feel a twinge of guilt about the times

145

when I thought of the friends and family I could perhaps have helped over the years. I always worried that I'd be seen as interfering, or in the way. Maybe this is a lesson for all of us to listen harder to young moms.

When Alex attended antenatal classes, PND was never even mentioned. When she took Anthony to be weighed and have his injections, she told the clinic sister she was struggling. 'Her suggestion was to call a new mother she knew who lived close to me to meet up. But when you're suffering from anxiety and depression, the last thing you have the mental strength to do is just call up a stranger and say, "Hey …".' She casts her eyes upwards.

'I remember being so lonely. I'd stopped going out anywhere because it always felt like everyone was staring at me when Anthony would start crying, besides which I was so tired and emotional it felt impossible to summon up enough courage and energy to get out. So I would spend the days pacing up and down inside our very hot house with Anthony on me in the sling, rarely seeing visitors. The visits were always awkward as I would be close to tears and constantly fussing over Anthony – it was never a nice chat with coffee on the couch. Towards the middle of the afternoon I would get so tired I don't know how I didn't trip over my own feet or collapse onto the floor. By evening I would move my pacing to the front window where I could see our driveway gate, watching it like a dog, waiting for Paul to get home so that I could have some company.'

With nothing else to occupy you other than the baby, and no one to share your fears, they simply build up until you're at boiling point.

'Anthony wasn't putting on the weight he should because the breastfeeding wasn't going so well – and once again,

146

having been told anyone can breastfeed, I didn't think to check if there was anything wrong with me, which it turned out there was. I only found out I had what's known as tuberous breasts when my second child Olivia was a year old. This defect meant that I didn't have enough breast tissue to make enough milk. With Anthony, I was just told you have to try harder and do more because there's no such thing as not having enough milk. By this point I had tried everything – demand feeding, hot showers, pumping, jungle juice, supplements, breast massage, diet changes, hot compresses on my breasts and Espiride capsules.

'When the clinic sister saw Anthony wasn't putting on weight she said I should start topping up his feed with a bottle. I took this as a personal failing. I wasn't enough for him – after all, everyone knew breast was best. The guilt and shame were piling on.

'This was one of the things that encouraged me to start the Mums Support Network after Olivia was born, and since then I've met so many women who also thought they were the only ones in this situation. There's massive pressure to breastfeed exclusively, which – despite popular belief – is not always the best option for a mother and child, as everyone's personal circumstances are different.

'When Anthony was six weeks old I realised I had no choice and had to give him top-up formula feeds and for the first time he started settling. Maybe the screaming had been from hunger, plus he was surely feeding off my anxiety. I was unsettled and so was he. Around then I went to my GP and told her I was struggling. She gave me some energy sachets which she said would perk me up.'

At Anthony's six-week check-up with the paediatrician,

when Alex asked for help, she was told to have a glass of wine in the evening, which would take the edge off: again, complete avoidance of the words 'postnatal depression', with alcohol possibly the worst and most dangerous escape route.

'At least now Anthony was getting into a bit of a routine and had started sleeping longer and didn't need to be on me quite so much. But instead of me sleeping when I put him down at night I found myself wide awake with my mind racing, sweating and with chest pains, lying there dreading every-thing about the next day. I didn't know what was happening but I knew this wasn't right. With no sleep I was permanently exhausted. If I did manage to sleep at all, I would wake up in the morning with a heavy, tight feeling in my chest, wondering how I was going to get through the day, even if it was a normal day with nothing planned. I was also anaemic, as part of my placenta had stayed in my uterus, so at six weeks I had to go for a D&C [dilation and curettage, the surgical removal of the contents of the uterus by scraping] done under a general anaes-thetic. Anthony was inconsolable in the hours he wasn't with me, which just sent me even further downhill, so by the time he was seven weeks old I was in total despair.'

Having told her story many times, she is able to tell it without reliving too much of the emotion. But in its place I sense a silent anger at the lack of help and support she received.

'Another visit to my GP for help saw me getting a mild antidepressant. This was like eating sweets for me and did absolutely nothing – partly because they take a few weeks to kick in. I now felt so desperate and knew something had to change. I wanted to shake the doctor and say, "Do something that will help *now*," because I knew what was going on in my head. I was so exhausted and my anxiety levels were so high

148

I was starting to get an electric feeling in my limbs. I couldn't think straight. I felt sick all the time and couldn't eat. The person I was had completely disappeared. Paul came from a family where he'd learnt to get on with things during the hard times and although now he fully understands PND, at the time he didn't.

'One day I was crying next to him, saying I wasn't coping. I was really struggling with this and I didn't want to be in a room alone with the baby as I'd become so scared of him. Paul said, "But he's just a baby, he hasn't done anything wrong – why can't you just love him?" Those words have stuck in my mind for the last nine years. They hurt so much. I wasn't doing any of this on purpose and would have done anything for it to be different. I was desperate to have a life where I loved this baby but instead I was making plans in my head to abandon him at my in-laws' house with some bottles and nappies, drive to the airport and go off to a new life – anywhere. I had to get out or die. I just knew it had to end now – I was close to breaking point,' says Alex, the emotion she felt at the time showing in her voice.

Sadly, what Alex didn't know was how common feelings like these were for new moms. Once she realised she wasn't alone, she knew she had to do something to stop other moms from going through this, which ultimately led her to form the Mums Support Network.

'Recently a couple of lovely photos taken by my sister of myself with Anthony at seven weeks popped up on my Facebook page. I looked at them and thought, *Do they look like two normal photos of a loving mother and content baby?* I find it very hard to look at those pictures. They remind me of all the feelings I was desperately trying to hide at the time. I smiled at

Anthony because I knew that's what a mother was supposed to do. It's what people watching me were expecting me to do, but I hated my life on the inside.'

There are certain expectations that society instils in women; your automatic bonding with your child is one of them. And it's not just women who have PND who go through this. There is ongoing research into why not all mothers automatically bond with their children and, while depression is often linked to this, there are exceptions.

'When Anthony was eight and a half weeks old it was our wedding anniversary. I remember going to bed that night not knowing what was happening to my body. I was catatonic, curled up in the foetal position, shaking and crying the whole night. When Paul tried to talk to me in the morning I was awake but couldn't move. I was trying to shut out the world from under the covers and he said okay, I'm going to make an appointment at the doctor but you have to get out of bed, have a shower and get dressed. The world seemed so terrifying I couldn't get up. I was staying where I was. I could barely get any words out so he physically had to get me out of bed, all the time talking to me like a small child, talking me through a shower, dressing me and trying to feed me. It was as though my brain said, I'm done – I can't do this any more. I'm just shutting off. I think it was either that or killing myself. I was like a robot, doing everything mechanically with no feeling. That day, our seventh wedding anniversary, was the day I was finally admitted into hospital.'

Alex was hospitalised for ten days. She did nothing but sleep for the first few days. 'I felt guilty because I was relieved to be away from Anthony and I wasn't missing him. I wasn't missing the whole home environment. I started seeing a psychiatrist

150

daily, but the day they said they were going to discharge me I remember feeling terrified about going back home. I thought this is my safe place now, people bring me food, look after me and all I have to do is just sit here. I don't have any responsibilities and now I am expected to go back and be a mother again.'

The psychiatrist put Alex on antidepressants, although these had to be changed several times over the next few weeks before they got them right – which saw Alex having a few ups and downs. The medical team also decided that it would be a good idea for Alex's mom to move in with them for a month when she came out of hospital, rather than her being alone with the baby – which really helped.

Antidepressants aren't a magic wand that waves over you to get rid of your depression. It often takes time and patience to find what works best for you.

'Just over a month later, we went away for a few days' holiday, not too far, and with Paul's family. I felt like I could handle that. I clearly remember sitting with Anthony when he started smiling and laughing at the funny faces Paul was pulling at him. I remember that was the first time I felt the dark clouds surrounding me lifting just ever so slightly and everything felt a bit lighter. The sun wasn't shining through yet, but I could breathe a little easier and the days stopped feeling like mountains to climb, which was the start of things slowly getting better and better.' I see and hear Alex's shift into a more comfortable place.

At last, there was a diagnosis. 'I was finally told I had PND, which I still couldn't quite believe, and that it was severe. I thought, *I'm not one of* those *mothers*. This of course is part of growing up in a society where the stigma around mental health is so huge. My dad had explained to my sister when I went into hospital that I'd had a nervous breakdown – a term you rarely hear today. I guess that's what it was and I just thought, *Am I mad? Am I crazy? Does this mean I'm unsafe to be around my baby? Will he be taken away from me?* This is a very common worry for mothers with PND, which makes them reluctant to admit it for fear of losing their baby.'

Once again, the stigma of mental health rears its ugly head. With the term 'nervous breakdown' and all its connotations gradually disappearing, perhaps one day the words 'crazy' and 'mad' will follow into disuse.

'I was now seeing a psychologist once a week and was in touch with the psychiatrist on the phone as we slowly got the medication right. But more than anything I felt a new me emerging, particularly with Anthony. When I look back to that particular day on holiday, I can even remember what he was wearing and almost the moment my brain connected. It's similar to the feeling you get when you're first attracted to someone – and from there, my feelings towards him started to grow. Instead of saying I can't face putting him to bed, I'm feeling too anxious, I'd say, "I think I can do it."

'It helped that at four months babies get more interactive, so Anthony and I started reacting to each other. He was smiling, gurgling and reacting to things I was doing. At the same time I started going to a mother-and-baby group once a week to give me a chance to get out of the house for a couple of hours and talk to other moms. I was lucky I was in a group with moms who were really down to earth and relaxed, which made it eas-ier to open up a little bit about things. Another group I went to was far more "cliquey" and, according to them, their babies all slept like little angels right through the night and had perfect daily routines. Not one of them mentioned anything negative about their mothering experience.'

For Alex, the first group opened many new doors. 'With the group I was in, I learnt different things to do with Anthony, which helped because I needed some sort of routine to make me feel more in control. We settled into a routine which worked for both of us, with him having his naps and me having some free time with bedtime at 7 pm. Bath time and massage time became quite relaxed – pleasant, even.

'Just getting through the day, though, was still quite tough, and I was relieved when his bedtime came. But I could pat myself on the back for managing to get through another day by myself. Part of my success was lowering my expectations. I planned to get through just one thing or less every day. So I'd either go to the shops or go for a walk, but not both together. I tried to do the bare minimum and made myself accept this was okay.

'From the April when we'd gone on holiday to the end of May was a huge turning point. I was finally on the right pill regime and really started enjoying my time with Anthony. Sometimes I'd feel a little jittery when I woke up but I knew it was nothing I couldn't handle. I even started to get back into an exercise routine, which of course added to my growing feelings of well-being.' Exercise: an important antidote to anything to do with depression or anxiety, but something that's not always achievable when you're feeling really down.

'As we'd decided I wouldn't go back to work but rather stay with Anthony and just do Paul's books, my mother and I chatted about the possibility of me starting a group for women who had gone through what I had. So I tried putting up a few posters but decided against calling it a PND support group but rather a group for moms having a hard time emotionally, as I

153

was aware that some would find the stigma of a PND group discouraging. When no one responded I shelved the idea, coming back to it when Anthony started going to a playgroup at two years old. This time, one person came, and she had gone through a similar experience to me. Basically, this was one-to-one counselling, which was good for both her and myself. But then she moved away and I fell pregnant with Olivia.'

Although Alex had planned another pregnancy, this time she didn't want the birth to be in January, with the painful memories of Anthony's birth hanging over her. But that was exactly what happened when she discovered she was pregnant in April, sending her into a slight panic. 'I also knew that my previous history of PND was a risk factor for the second time around, so I knew I had to do all I could to avoid it. Naively, I thought that I could avoid it … I thought seeing a therapist during my pregnancy would help and just before Olivia arrived we employed a full-time maid and an au pair for a couple of hours in the afternoon when Anthony came home from playschool. By the time Anthony had turned one and a half I'd been weaned off my antidepressants and instead of feeling anxious about Olivia's birth I was really excited, particularly because I'd always wanted a boy first and a daughter second. People told me that girls are much easier, and that she'd be very different. I thought the only way it could be worse would be if this baby had terrible colic and screamed even more than Anthony. But I knew the chances were that it would be better, and it was,' she says, her relief coming through loud and clear.

'Again, I wanted a natural birth, but as she was a footling breach and her little feet were dancing on her umbilical cord, I had to have a Caesarean. One of my best friends is an anaesthetist so she did my spinal block, which for a control freak like me meant a far more peaceful birth which I felt was totally under control. It was a happy day, with people laughing and joking and a totally different atmosphere from Anthony's frantic birth. Everything went well and, after coming out screaming, she stopped and became calm. She was pronounced a perfectly healthy baby. Right from the start, Olivia's character was completely different to Anthony's, which it still is. As I'd had a Caesar they kept her in the nursery at night to let me sleep as part of my recovery and then brought her to me only for night feeds and again in the morning. I'd look at her and think, *I wonder if I could just go to the loo and eat my breakfast before I feed her?* She'd just lie there, quite peacefully. This was so much easier and this time around I wasn't afraid to ask questions and ask the staff for help. I'd also decided to stay in hospital for as long as I could.'

As they hadn't yet discovered her tuberous breast problem, Alex found breastfeeding Olivia difficult but she did seem to be getting just enough. 'Once I was back home things did start getting a bit hectic after a few weeks and by four weeks Paul and I were snapping at each other all the time and once again I felt my anxiety building – although not to the previous levels. We had a family meeting and I went to see a psychiatrist, after which we all decided that the best thing would be for me to stop breastfeeding and go on the same medications that had worked with Anthony. We stopped PND in its tracks, as it were,' says Alex proudly.

This just proves that, armed with the right information and support, no one has to go through this ordeal.

'I still feel guilty because I often think maybe I could have breastfed her a little longer, but for the well-being of all of us I think I made the right decision to switch to bottle feeding.

After this, things went back to being calm and controlled again. And then there's the whole natural vs Caesarean issue, which at the time seemed such a big deal.

'Now I look at my six- and nine-year-old, one who was a natural birth and the other a Caesar, and can I see any difference between them in terms of development, health or intelligence? Absolutely not! I also see some of my friends who had home water births and breastfed exclusively, and their children have the same problems as mine, if not more.

'People were right, though, about the second time around being so much easier and I did feel a lot more relaxed. I learnt to lower my expectations and not put so much pressure on myself. For instance, if we were going out I didn't make a fuss if it was over her nap time, whereas with Anthony I was driven by a strict schedule.'

Once Olivia was older and had begun attending a playgroup, Alex found she had a couple of free mornings so decided once again to start a mums' support group, but this time 'to do it properly'. 'Like many stay-at-home moms, I was struggling to find a purpose. You're not bringing in a salary – you're not getting a lot of validation from your children. Your day consists of changing nappies, making food and singing songs. For most new mothers, that's a battle. At the same time, I had my lawyer husband coming home, telling me about solving multimillion-dollar cases and then asking about my day, which always sounded quite pathetic in comparison.'

A new baby and an older child will certainly keep you busy, but sometimes you need something more to give you back your sense of self-worth and deflect loneliness or anxiety. For Alex, this was forming her support group.

'Even though I know that motherhood is the most important

job in the world, somehow it just didn't cut it for me. I also knew there was no support group in Durban for mothers with PND or mothers who were struggling in general with that transition from woman to mother. After having some conversations with mothers, I realised they needed a space where they felt safe to admit their struggles, without feeling judged. Even without PND this is still a major change in a woman's life, which many mothers have to get through alone without having a space to admit it. They would go on to social media to see #soblessed with photos of glowing moms with spotlessly clean houses and immaculately turned out babies and children.'

Aware of the stigma attached to the words 'postnatal depression', Alex decided to rather call her group Mums Support Network, making it clear that it was open to any mom struggling or feeling lonely, isolated, depressed, or anything that was making her unhappy.

'I went to my GP and some baby clinics, and put some ads up on Facebook, spreading the word to friends and acquaintances who'd just had babies. We had the first meeting when Olivia was two in September 2016 in my lounge, where I got my own psychologist to come and give a little talk to attract a few more people. I told SADAG as well and got some great advice from them on the do's and don'ts of running these meetings.

'In order to put some distance between my personal life and the support group, I found a lady who had a little cafe which she only used for parties at weekends and who was happy for us to use it for our meetings. Armed with our own refreshments, we moved in and from then on the group grew and grew. I started realising how many moms need this kind of space where they can speak openly and without judgement, which is the most important thing with our groups.

'And it's totally confidential – what happens in the room stays in the room and everyone knows they won't be judged. One of the moms said she loves this space because if you're a mother and you're suicidal, people will have a lot of sympathy for you but she was considering killing her baby because of PND and how could she tell anyone that? People aren't going to have any sympathy – they're just going to think you're a monster, whether it's the illness or not.'

For Hayley Lieberthal, meeting Alex was life-changing. When she fell pregnant with her first child, she knew there was a possibility of PND in her future as her mom had gone through this with Hayley herself.

'When this happened it was a big shock. Pregnancy is supposed to be such a happy time but behind my smile was sadness. I'd always wanted to be a mom and, as a qualified playschool teacher seeing other moms and their tots, I couldn't understand what was wrong with me. Luckily for me my husband was really supportive and understanding as was my family, particularly my mom who knew what I was going through.

'After I had my daughter and brought her home, as the key turned in our front door the anxiety and fear kicked in. Luckily for me, someone in my Jewish community arrived with a mitzvah meal, and as she wished me mazeltov on my baby, I broke down. I didn't know this woman at all, but for some reason I felt safe with her and she told me about Mums Support Network and that I should come to the next meeting.

'This was when I met Alexandra. She came outside to greet me and gave me this warm welcoming hug. Mums Support Network became a ray of light – all of a sudden here's other moms saying all these things I identified with. Suddenly I realised it's not just me going through this, which made me feel so much better.

'Although I had support from my family, nobody talks about the reality of motherhood and you are going to question yourself. We're too afraid to say certain things normally but when you're in Mums Support Network people really listen to you, without judgement.

'Being part of this organisation means I can help to see that other moms never go through what I did. I hope in the near future to fall pregnant again and this time around I'm so much more prepared, knowing what to expect and how to recognise the signs sooner.

'When a mom speaks out on what they're going through, instead of being told, "You can't say that," at Mums Support Network you're more likely to hear, "I'm so sorry you're going through this. You're having a rough time. Perhaps I could watch your kids for a while and you can have a break." The empathy, support and encouragement are incredible. Instead of being told, "Snap out of it," we help women to understand and handle what they're going through, which is a very real thing. For me to give my time to helping other women in similar situations to me is a great way to help break the stigma, around not just PND but also depression and anxiety.'

One area Alex is passionate about is changing the attitudes of medical professionals towards PND. 'When you fall pregnant in South Africa, doctors hardly ever mention mental health and women already on antidepressants are often wrongly encouraged to stop taking them. Gynaecologists' focus is on your physical health. Importantly, for our physical and mental health needs, we need to make regular contact with other women. That old saying of it takes a village to raise a child is so true and at Mums Support Network we're trying to bring back that village of support.'

TOOLBOX TIPS

For mothers and mothers-to-be

- ❏ If you're not coping, don't be ashamed to seek help. This isn't your fault, and it can't be fixed by 'trying harder' or 'staying positive'. It's believed that PND affects more than one in three women, and is often unreported – you're not alone.
- ❏ If you're not sure you have PND, don't suffer in silence. Chat to someone you trust, your GP, a close family member, a clinic sister, a religious advisor or a friend. If you're struggling in any way, ask for help.
- ❏ Taking medication for PND doesn't make you a failure or weak. PND is a medical condition that causes a chemical imbalance in the brain which can be corrected with the correct medication. You won't turn into a zombie or become an unfit parent, and it doesn't mean you're crazy. It means you're brave. It's safe to take certain medication for PND while pregnant and while breastfeeding.
- ❏ Treatment can be a combination, or all, of the following: therapy (seeing a psychologist), medication and group support.
- ❏ Remember self-care. Put yourself first. You can't fill someone else's cup if your own is empty. Self-care includes good nutrition, exercise, a good sleep environment, supportive friends, time spent in nature.
- ❏ Lower your own standards and expectations. Don't be so hard on yourself. This job is not easy, and you're doing great.

- PND is 100 per cent treatable. With the correct help, mothers will make a full recovery. However, if left untreated it can be fatal. If you're having hallucinations, hearing voices, or having intrusive thoughts about harming yourself or your child, seek medical attention immediately. You'll be helped, not judged.

For concerned family and friends

- It can be difficult to tell whether a mother is battling. Societal pressure to look like the perfect mother will probably lead to her saying something like, 'I'm doing okay! I'm so blessed. I'm loving every minute.' Ask her how she's *really* getting on. It's easy to hide the despair and emptiness behind the happy facade.
- If someone you love has PND, it's not something you can fix by yourself. Get professional help. You can't support her on your own; doing so will take its toll on you, too.
- Living with someone who has PND is hard. She'll be unreasonable, irrational, angry, needy … but it's not her. And she isn't upset with you. It's the illness. Don't take it personally. It takes patience and compassion; you may also need psychological help and support to get through this.

161

8

AJ VENTER

Anxiety disorder

Picture a handsome, rugged, masculine South African, and then add the word 'Springbok'. What you get is AJ Venter, whose superb rugby career earned him 26 caps for his Springbok appearances worldwide. Does this sound like someone who could doubt himself or find himself in a situation of sheer panic? After all, in South Africa the 'manne' are strong and the words 'mental health' don't apply to guys like AJ Venter – until they did, when in 2015 AJ's life came crashing down, putting him on a path that would change his life but ultimately turn into a better new normal.

Born into an idyllic life on a Karoo sheep farm in the Free State, AJ's future was sealed the minute his father handed him his first rugby ball at the tender age of four. He was to grow into a 1.98-metre teenager, whose speed belied his build, just waiting to be snapped up by a major club. Indeed, his long career saw him playing for all of South Africa's premier rugby clubs except the Bulls, with his longest stint being with the Sharks for 12 years. The call to join the Springboks in November 2000 was naturally a highlight in his career.

'People have asked me over the years what it felt like to run onto the pitch in the green and gold, whether there were nerves and pressure involved – but there weren't. Playing rugby for me was always easy, and when you're doing what you love, no work is too hard and no game is too tough. As you grow you become better and stronger, and then one day you're playing in front of 70 000 people and it's just like it would be for anyone else – another day at the office. I tried not to focus on the crowds in the stands once I was on the pitch but solely on the other 29 people on the field. Once that whistle blew there was nothing else for me – just the game.'

Rugby gave AJ opportunities that very few kids from his background would have had, such as finding himself in a town 60 kilometres outside Venice at the age of 22, learning not just the Italian language but a whole new culture. 'I was really grateful for this opportunity. For a boy from the Free State this was mind-blowing for me, and I left three years later with a very different outlook on life and an Italian girlfriend who went on to become my wife. Rugby gave me so much, but what it doesn't prepare you for is what to do when your career is over. So much time is given to practice that these days there's almost no time to study for a "backup" career.'

With this in mind, by the time AJ was 36 he decided that rather than wait for his game to deteriorate he'd go out while he was still considered a top player. 'I count myself lucky to have played for so long, even though I could have played for another year or two. I knew, though, that I really needed to get into the business world, and the older I became the harder that would be, especially as I had no business training. A lot of the other guys I played with had decided to end their careers playing in Europe and earning good money. I decided to spend that time developing contacts and forming business relationships in my off-time, preparing to leave rugby. When my team mates went to play golf, I went to work and learn, not for money but just to spend time with friends in businesses, attending meetings with them, understanding how they worked, so at least I'd have some knowledge before going into business.

'Nothing, though, can prepare you for that transformation. As a rugby player even in your early 30s, playing at a certain level you get well paid, people adore you and there are always beautiful women around. You don't look further than tomorrow or the next year and the world is your oyster. Then suddenly you're in the real world and it's a very different one, although my reputation did lead me into an interesting learning experience with a bank as my first job. My name opened a lot of doors for them, as they worked with high-level clients, and once those doors were open their more experienced sales guys could do the rest. But I learnt each day, soaking up how they worked.'

After working in similar positions for another couple of years, AJ felt he was ready to jump into his own business, which he did, quickly learning that it wasn't as easy as it looked. With a transport business followed by an online real-estate business seeing AJ losing a considerable amount of money, he realised that perhaps he'd been a little too quick to leave the banking environment. Added to this, he'd had two failed marriages and a four-year relationship that had also ended.

'These relationships and the business failures weighed heavily on me and made me doubt myself. I doubted my ability to have a successful relationship because of these repeated failures. On top of this the pressures of finance and money were also starting to weigh on me. After breaking up with my last girlfriend I suddenly began to think, I'm getting older and would I ever be able to have children. This had never been an issue for me before, as it had for many of my friends. I wondered if I was pretending to myself when I said I didn't care about having kids. With all these thoughts circulating in my head I started to become more and more anxious.'

These thoughts gradually consume your every waking moment and, without professional help, can easily take over your mind. For AJ, these types of thoughts went with being weak – something that wasn't in his vocabulary.

AJ dismissed these feelings of anxiety. After all, everyone has their problems and deals with them – don't they? This is the stigma that stops us questioning what our hearts and minds, and often our bodies, are telling us – that we need help. If someone like AJ felt that any part of his body wasn't working to maximum fitness, he'd have done something about it immediately. But, like most people, his mental health wasn't a consideration then.

'My reasoning was that not many people are totally happy with their lives and I must just deal with everything and carry on. By 2015 I found myself getting a little worse every week when it came to anxiety. I also started noticing how miserable I felt each week as the weekend drew near, with me having no real plans as most of my friends were now married, had kids and were involved in family time. This was of course all in my head as any of them would have had me around with open arms. But we refute those thoughts in our heads and start honing in on the negative ones. As the weeks went on and each weekend came closer the anxiety would start building, until one week it kicked in already by the Tuesday. That Friday I woke with sweaty palms, a heavy head and aching body, as though I'd had too much to drink the night before. I didn't feel in control of my body, which for me felt really weird.'

With anxiety attacks, there are rarely warning signs in the form of small attacks building up to a larger one. When an anxiety attack hits, it generally hits hard – as it did with AJ.

'By 3 that afternoon I felt the walls in my apartment closing in on me and I felt dreadful. I wasn't sure if I was having a heart attack, a stroke, or what was happening to me. An hour later and rapidly feeling worse, I called my doctor as I knew he'd shortly be going off for the weekend and I needed help. Once he heard my symptoms he told me he thought I was having an anxiety attack or a nervous breakdown. Once we agreed that I could drive myself to the pharmacy he sent them a prescription for me to collect some medication. Somehow I got there and immediately took two of the prescribed pills. Within a couple of hours I was feeling much better and later that night took two more. For the first time in months I had a really good sleep.

'The next morning I took two more and was still feeling good and again I had a great night's sleep. I looked at these pills and decided that I should find out just what I was taking. I've always tried to follow the natural route and never been one to take medication so I googled the name and saw they were antidepressants and I was a bit shocked. Me, depressed? So I decided not to take them that Sunday morning, it just didn't feel right for me, but very shortly after, the anxiety came back full-on. I knew I could take the medication and I'd feel better again but I decided that rather than mask my symptoms I wanted to try and fix the problem.

'Sitting there that morning one name came into my head: Allan Kleynhans, who was our motivational coach when I was at the Sharks. Since then he'd become an internationally renowned speaker and motivational coach. I'd kept in touch with him through Facebook over the years and knew he lived in the UK so I sent him a Facebook message telling him what I was going through and that I really needed to talk to him. He immediately got back to me but said he would only be able to talk to me the following Wednesday because he was working in Eastern Europe. That was a long time to wait but somehow I got through it, and from the Wednesday we started doing two-hour Skype sessions speaking about how I was feeling and guiding me on what I should try to do.'

What so many people don't realise is the power of simply being able to talk to someone about what's going on in your life. The word 'therapy', particularly in South Africa, still carries a stigma, whereas in many other countries it's as normal as going for dental check-ups and far less stressful. There's a point in almost every interview about mental health I've done at which I can see a person's body language and face relax as they talk about having found someone to talk to.

'We covered so many different things, looking back at the pressures I was feeling over failed marriages, businesses … He explained these were just thoughts and made me see that maybe I didn't have all the money in the world but I wasn't going to die. I was going to live, but by giving those negative thoughts space in my head I was giving fuel to my anxiety. For each moment I'd spent thinking like this the thoughts became bigger in my mind.'

This is at the crux of anxiety issues that we've all had, especially during times like the Covid-19 pandemic; at night, in particular, thoughts go around in your head, escalating into mammoth problems.

'Although I lived in a beautiful apartment, had a car, friends and my health, in my mind I didn't see any of those things. All I saw was that other people had better apartments, bigger cars and great families. I didn't see the underlying things – what I had to be grateful for. It's like if you decide to buy a Toyota Hilux and you start researching Hiluxes on AutoTrader and looking at different websites. Suddenly every time you drive down the road you see Toyota Hiluxes. It's not as though suddenly there's more of these vehicles on the road – they've always been there but now my focus is open to obsessively seeing that brand.

'When the pressure starts building we start focusing only on those negative things and stop focusing on the good things in life. You just see dark clouds and hardship, to the extent for me where I went from never having a sleep problem to going through nights of no sleep. I also went from my rugby weight of 115 kilograms to 94 kilograms in a short time. Although I'd always exercised, I was now doing it to excess. I learnt that stress can manifest itself in your body and if you don't change the stress nothing else can change. Research even shows this could be a contributing factor to many serious illnesses – it's where your mind can affect your body and I certainly saw this in myself.'

AJ was at a turning point, and his life now took a massive swing. From obsessing about everything he didn't have and what had gone wrong, he began focusing on what was positive in his life and what lay ahead. After all, he was in his early 40s and had a whole life filled with possibilities ahead.

'At first my sessions with Allan were quite draining. I remember that for the first hour I just cried – I couldn't speak and he was just there listening and slowly guiding me in different directions. The main thing was to start training my mind to identify my triggers so when I started to feel anxious, even in the middle of the night, I could identify what was setting this off. Was it money, relationships? Once I'd identified it then I'd immediately say, "I respect you" and try in my mind to put it aside and focus on something I should be grateful for. This could be something as simple as the fresh fruit in my fridge, my phone, computer, house or friends. I had to start reminding myself of all the good things I'd forgotten about.

'This didn't happen overnight and took quite a few months where I had to be really diligent and strict with myself before it started happening naturally. Even after almost three years I was still having some negative thoughts but now my mind could start eliminating them quicker, letting me focus on the positive, which was what really helped me. It's like a muscle that doesn't work properly unless you exercise it. I only had about five sessions with Allan but he'd put me on this path and showed me how to go further.'

AJ started researching other top motivational coaches, learning as he went. 'One of the things that has helped me enormously was learning to meditate, something I do every day with a particular emphasis on what I must be grateful for. For me it's not a religious experience as it is for some people, but it helps me identify and appreciate the small things in life, particularly in this social media world where you're bombarded with how wonderful everyone's so-called perfect life is. Suddenly you realise that's not important – it's about how full of good things your life is, how lucky you are to have all these things.'

One of the reasons mental health still carries a stigma is simply historical. Previously, you had to just take whatever life threw at you and simply carry on. Today, with just a little research you can discover so many wonderful ways to enhance your life without looking too far.

Since then, AJ has come a long way. He has started a new business and become a motivational speaker, talking about his experiences. Whenever he speaks at a corporate event or a conference, people – particularly men – come up to him to share their similar experiences and, often, to ask for advice. 'People can sense I've really opened myself up and they can relate to someone who's vulnerable, especially if they feel the same.'

A real turning point was in March 2020 when he spoke on national television about overcoming his anxiety. Suddenly he started receiving calls from friends and acquaintances who shared their similar stories, often seeking help. 'So many of my friends called me, telling me what had happened to them and how lost they'd felt. It's a little embarrassing to talk about at first. We're conditioned to think you've got to succeed in life – you can't be weak, which is also where the stigma comes in, making it hard for people to open up about their mental health problems.

'When I first decided to start marketing my talks on social media platforms I did a little video about my story, which I saved on my computer for months before I finally pressed the button and it was online. I knew the minute I pressed that button there was no going back but somehow I felt great relief in this vulnerability, which in itself is a way of healing. I don't have to hide it any more. In fact, now it's easy to talk about it freely.'

Today, AJ is a picture of health and it's rare that you'll hear him sounding anything but positive. 'I've realised there's so much more to life than what we think. If I was drawing a graph of my life it would show a gradual upward incline in satisfaction with occasional hardships but nothing dramatic until anxiety overcame me, then the curve would go in a straight line downwards. That was where talking to Allan and learning so much about getting myself and my life back on track came in. Right now I'm at the top of the graph in business and my spiritual life – and, I hope, in being a good friend again.

'Today I'm opening myself up to different religions and life outlooks. There's a whole new world I've never seen and would never have looked at without going through this difficult time. Today I don't just see a narrow slice of life, with all its hardships – now I have a 360-degree view.'

TOOLBOX TIPS

Understand the cycle of anxiety

- ❏ Nobody knows what will happen in the future, no one can change the past, and there are many situations no one can control. Paying too much attention to these often results in anxiety.
- ❏ Making predictions and assumptions that aren't necessarily true and are often negative can also result in anxiety.

All people experience all feelings

- ❏ If people could control how they felt, they'd never feel sad, for example. This puts difficult feelings into the mix, like frustration, guilt or shame, and increases their worries.
- ❏ People don't like acknowledging or expressing difficult feelings like anxiety. They judge themselves or avoid the feelings. This doesn't work, and can even make things worse.

171

- ❏ The more you keep things inside, the more overwhelmed you become.
- ❏ Sharing how you feel gives others an opportunity to do the same. The more we share, the more we can support one another and lessen anxiety.

Acceptance means accepting the situation and the feelings you have about it

- ❏ Many people acknowledge that situations are out of their control, try to accept this, and move on, but they mistakenly believe that accepting a situation means not having feelings about it.
- ❏ Accepting a situation means accepting the feelings that arise as a result.

Getting help doesn't mean you're weak

- ❏ Mental illnesses aren't a test of strength – they're illnesses.
- ❏ It's okay not to be okay. It takes strength to seek help, but doing so will leave you feeling much stronger, in control and capable of dealing with life.

Learn to notice your thoughts: they're not always true or helpful

- ❏ Our thoughts are often untrue, unfair, or unhelpful. They're biased. It's essential to notice them, without unknowingly accepting them as truths, to gain perspective. We can control how we react to thoughts. Learn how to control what you pay attention to through mindfulness.

172

❏ Speaking to someone is extremely helpful for gaining perspective. Writing about how you feel helps you view your thoughts more clearly.

9

YVETTE HESS

Bipolar disorder

When I first started writing about mental health, like many others I thought that bipolar disorder was an extreme type of depression. This is probably because people with bipolar disorder have depressive episodes, which are often quite extreme. The difference is that, in depression, the lows – as in Melissa's story – are more than just lows. There's a deep sadness or emptiness that stays with you, along with the other symptoms mentioned in her chapter. But in bipolar disorder, the highs reach the point of mania. Yvette's story shows these extreme mood swings: 'bipolar' itself refers to the opposite poles of the emotional spectrum, the highs (mania) and the lows (depression).

When you hear that someone has bipolar disorder, what picture do you get in your mind? Given that this illness was previously called manic depression, you might think about someone who is a bit off the wall. But one thing I've learnt as a journalist who has covered mental health for many years is that the picture you form before meeting someone is often completely wrong.

This was certainly the case with Yvette Hess. I knew she'd had bipolar disorder for many years, and that her journey through this difficult illness had been a traumatic one. Being a mom of three young boys alone is enough to tire you out. So when she arrives for our interview bursting with energy and enthusiasm, excited to tell her story, I immediately realise that my initial expectation of a slightly nervous, tired woman is completely wrong. Not only that, here is a woman who is prepared, for the sake of reaching people with her story, to be incredibly open and honest about her journey.

'I knew I was different as a child,' Yvette begins. 'At least I felt I was. I didn't look different but somehow I felt detached, as if I didn't belong. The problem was I didn't know then how to express this, especially within the tight-knit coloured community I grew up in. Moving to the Free State when I was seven in 1993, and becoming the only coloured child in my school, certainly didn't help – because that made me stand apart and validated my negative feelings about myself.'

Having spoken a few times to Yvette on the phone, and now sitting opposite her, I haven't even thought of race. But for Yvette, in her youth it was a big part of who she was and what formed her.

Another formative experience for Yvette was a hidden secret. '1993 was also the year my childhood was irretrievably stolen from me,' she continues. 'It was a normal day in a normal week but what was different was that my parents left my younger sister and me in the care of a close friend who was visiting us. That day, the day I was sexually molested, is indelibly marked in my mind. It didn't happen in a flash but was drawn out, with us "playing games" for what seemed like endless hours. I knew what we were doing was wrong – terribly wrong – but I'd been brought up to be polite and respect adults. I was also a chronic pleaser so had no idea I could even say no. He'd also said if I

175

told anyone I'd then be blamed for breaking up the family and I couldn't think of carrying such a burden. All I remember thinking was that my little sister, who was busy watching cartoons on TV, mustn't be drawn into this. Protecting her was my main thought, so later in the day when he tried to entice her to sit on the couch with him under a blanket, a real fear set in. I said no, leave her, take me instead. Luckily her friend arrived and she went outside to play. I'd felt dirty when he started doing these things and now I felt even dirtier.'

I feel the tension in the air forming around us as she speaks. This is not something you can discuss easily – especially with a stranger.

'That night, when I went to bed, I had what could be called an out-of-body experience of seeing what wasn't really there. But to me, seeing Casper the Friendly Ghost was very real. He was right there by my bed with other members of his family trying to make me laugh. I've since found out this is a standard way children deal with trauma but, together with the abuse, I also kept this to myself.

'What also left me in shock was realising that people you and your parents trusted could betray you in such a hideous way. How could I ever trust an adult again?'

You maybe nodding as you read this, having had similar experiences. This, sadly, is a story I've heard over and over again, with different outcomes for different people but with one common thread – children are scared to tell their parents, who often don't believe them. The result? Many lives affected over many years. People also rarely associate mental health with young children, but good mental health is important at any stage in life. It is best to be aware, listen and do something, and never to dismiss a child's sudden change in demeanour as moodiness.

Yvette was about 12 when she was first introduced to the internet, and the porn sites in her cousin's search history. Naturally curious, she opened the links.

'I knew what that man had done to me was very wrong but the pleaser in me knew how much pleasure I'd given him and I wanted to know if that was my job and duty.

'My parents soon discovered I'd been on those sites and naturally were angry and shocked – why was I doing this? I knew it was a result of what happened to me and for the first time I related the story of my abuse to them. I could see my mother believed me but to my surprise and horror my father didn't. That really hurt me but I later realised he was, in fact, disappointed in himself for trusting this man.

'As usual when there was a crisis in my family, my aunt, a psychologist, was called in. As child abuse was her speciality she soon discovered that this man had a number of cases against him and asked if I wanted to take it further. I could see the distress this was already causing my parents and I wondered what it would be like in court when I had to reveal the details of what had happened. I thought of the torment this would cause my parents and decided not to take it further. If I'd been older when I was asked this the answer would have been different. Today's court system is much easier, but then there was very little support for the abused child.'

I can hear the anger in Yvette's voice; the cry of an unheard child is still there.

'After my father had taken it all in, his first reaction was that he wanted to kill this man – which of course he said in pure anger. I didn't want him to be like that. My aunt managed to organise therapy for me, which helped, but a lot of damage had already been done.

'This experience of being molested had a massive impact on me and guided everything going forward in my life, from my choice of men to the type of friendships I had. It also impacted on the way I protected my sister, who was three years younger than me, and how I treated my family.'

Yvette felt almost as though 'part of her brain broke off' after this experience, leaving her emotions raw. To add to this, she felt that there was no one who could really understand what she was feeling and going through. For many children, this is a point where they break away into their own world – one Yvette knew well. [The Teddy Bear Clinic provides specialised help for young children who have experienced sexual abuse; no child should go through this alone. See www.ttbc.org.za.]

'I'd always been sensitive, but after this experience I became a super-sensitive child. Now I felt broken, so every sore became a lot more intense. My father couldn't understand why I'd cry over something that appeared trivial to him. For instance, if someone walked past me unexpectedly I'd jump, for seemingly nothing. I also found myself tearful much of the time, which looking back was possibly the start of my depression, together with the teen hormones which were kicking in – a recipe for disaster.

'From being what was termed a quiet child, I now found myself becoming very vocal when I was frustrated and almost got kicked out of the house a few times. I had an attitude problem, which I think was linked to trying to understand what was happening inside me. I wasn't dealing well with the effects of the trauma linked to the sexual abuse.'

The one place where Yvette was happy was at school, where she'd always excelled. Here, she could disappear into her books, which led her into different worlds. 'I also thought that, as I'd disappointed my dad with the sexual-abuse revelation, I'd make him and my mom proud by giving them good grades. I took this goal very seriously, earning the title of over-achiever. I became involved in many areas of school life, from Voortrekkers to scholar patrol. This went on throughout my school and varsity days, and pretty much up to today. Keeping busy and involved has always made me feel good.'

For someone who understands bipolar disorder, this almost manic behaviour would have been a red flag – but unfortunately for Yvette, as for many others, there was no one to pick this up. Had she had a muscle in her body that gave problems, for example, or a bad chest infection, it would have received immediate attention. An area that even today is still lacking in schools is not only the availability of therapists, but ones whom children feel are accessible and whom they can trust with their deepest thoughts. Luckily for Yvette, her school offered this service. They weren't perfect, but those early therapy sessions played a big role in her life.

'It was apparent, even in primary school, that I needed therapy and later we had therapy for family issues, specifically around the sexual abuse. Before my parents even knew about this I'd confided in the school therapist as I knew they couldn't tell anyone. Unfortunately this wasn't always the same person, so I didn't feel I had a confidante but I could at least offload and not be judged, which helped. That's why when I hear anyone else battling with everyday issues, I recommend they see a therapist.

'Although I saw a therapist all the way through my school career, the words "clinical depression" were never used, nor was medication ever mentioned.'

After leaving school, with her father's encouragement

179

Yvette enrolled part-time at the Vaal Triangle University to study accountancy – not that she had a real interest in this, but she thought it would lead to a good job. And again, she'd be pleasing her dad ...

'I was also working at ArcelorMittal as a clerk but my real passion was in anything creative. Once, I'd told my father I wanted to be an artist, and apart from looking disappointed he immediately told me how poor artists were! That's when I'd looked in the *Sunday Times* careers section and saw chartered accountancy jobs, and with my inbred struggle mentality I decided as I was good at accounting, this would be a good move.'

It wasn't long before the hyperactive thoughts kicked in once again, seeing Yvette caught up in extra-curricular activities. 'I'd organised a dance company to come to perform for the students at my campus and immediately caught the dance bug. This, I decided, was where I was meant to be. Without leaving my day job and while still studying at night, I took on the bookkeeping for the dance company as well as dancing with them during weekends. We'd travel around the country, dancing in different venues. I loved every minute, the makeup, costumes and the travel.' Yvette's passion for this is clear in the tone of her voice and the gestures of her arms as she speaks.

'This double life ended up seeing my stress levels go sky high. Even at 19 I had a lot of responsibility at my day job, working with huge numbers and budgets, when all I wanted was to dance all day. Some days I'd find myself at the SABC at 6 am dancing on *Morning Live*, and then return to the office with a face full of makeup and a batch of accounts to go through. Naturally, I crashed. Although I loved the high, I discovered the crash was inevitable,' she says with a deep sigh, now knowing the tell-tale signs she didn't know then.

This is classic bipolar behaviour. But if you don't recognise the signs, you'd just put it down to having a lot of energy, which appears to be part of who Yvette is – so why wouldn't she have an off-day now and then? At least that's what those who knew her thought. The crash was coming.

Yvette started dating one of the dancers in the company. Even though he was 15 years her senior, she describes him as 'like a child' and ended up supporting him. What she didn't realise was that she was forming a pattern of behaviour in her life that kept repeating itself.

'I was the one who desperately needed support, but didn't realise it then. All I saw was this attractive singer and dancer who was interested in me and for the next two years we were a couple. I never told him about my struggles with mental health and somehow he never asked about my fluctuating moods. Maybe he just thought it was premenstrual tension each month.'

Once again, Yvette knew her father was disappointed in her – she'd dropped out of varsity and her life now centred on dance. And again, she felt the familiar sense of failure. But this time, the answer for her was obvious. As we get to this part of her story, I see for the first time a more serious side of her as the story stirs up difficult memories.

'I decided I'd just take a lot of pills and fade into oblivion. The night I decided to do this I knew would be my last, so unusually for me I asked my dad if he'd like tea – something I'd never normally do. I knew it would be the last cup I'd ever make and went to great lengths to get it just right. After this I asked my sister if she'd sleep in my bed with me, which was also unusual for me. She didn't think anything of this and said

181

sure. The night before this I'd even initiated sex with my boy-friend, again something I didn't normally do.

'Before bed I sat down and wrote a letter explaining that I felt like a failure, didn't want to be a burden and a liability, so I was leaving … Then I went in search of every pill I could find that mentioned coma in the contraindications. I didn't really want to die. I just wanted to sleep and silence this feeling of failure, being different and detached, unable to connect with people. It was almost as though there was a glass wall and everyone on the other side was able to connect with each other and I was outside shouting, "Can you hear me – can you see me?"

'I knew when they found out what I did they'd be surprised. After all, "she made me tea", "we had sex" and "she asked to sleep next to me". But they didn't hear the cry for help. I needed somebody to help me but didn't know what this would look like. I thought at the back of my mind that one of them would think something's not right here. Her behaviour is out of the ordinary – what's up?'

The last thing Yvette's family would think was that there could be something wrong with her mentally, particularly when she was such a high achiever. All her family could think when they found her, with the letter, was to get her to hospital as fast as possible. There she was made to throw up the pills. The raw throat this left her with made it impossible for her to answer her family's desperate questions. And when it came to the nursing staff, there was little sympathy.

'My father had already quizzed my boyfriend in the waiting room on whether I was pregnant or if we'd had a fight. The hostility from the hospital staff was not what I needed then. They told me I should be locked up because I attempted to kill someone – myself. I don't think this situation has changed much and would really hope that nursing staff would be taught some sensitivity and compassion in this area.

'After this, I saw a psychiatrist for the first time. He said, "Yvette, you have two sides to you. Not a split personality, but sometimes you're very happy and other times you're very sad and these pills will help you with that." They said I had a dissociative disorder and even though I still had visions similar to the one of Casper the Friendly Ghost, which helped me cope, this diagnosis didn't seem right to me. I felt he'd given me certain puzzle pieces, but they didn't make a whole. I saw him for a few sessions, after which he said that was enough but to continue with therapy. I didn't understand the treatment programme, how the medication, therapy and everything fitted together with the psychiatry.'

I hear the frustration in her voice as she tells me this. If someone had taken the time and had the patience to explain what was wrong with Yvette, her future would have been very different. Doctors often treat patients as less than deserving of a full explanation. Unless patients insist on more, it's unlikely they'll get it – another reason for education about mental health. If someone says they feel pains running down their left arm and in their chest, almost everyone would know these are the classic signs of a heart attack. But 'feeling down' or 'being super energetic/high' doesn't ring alarm bells.

'While I was in the hospital recovering from the overdose there was a lady in the bed next to me who was a life coach. She went on to have a positive impact on my life, teaching me about meditation, building good habits, setting goals and how to get my mind and body right to achieve these goals. I battled with the meditation as I found it hard to still my mind. This was possibly because of the medication.

183

'When I left the hospital I carried on taking these meds and after a while I felt so much better I decided I didn't need them any more. I couldn't have been more wrong.' Yvette puts her hands to her head as she says this.

This is the number one mistake for people diagnosed with bipolar disorder. They feel 'fine'; they really miss those manic highs, and have forgotten about the deep lows. Soon, it was back to the cycle of self-destruction for Yvette.

'After I left the hospital I wanted to break off with my boyfriend – but instead I fell pregnant, which I didn't realise until I was almost four months pregnant. I saw this as a sign from God that I must stay with this man. This was the worst thing I could have done for my mental health. I was battling being in the wrong space with the wrong person. What I thought was love at the time was, of course, infatuation.

'By then I was off the pills and wasn't having therapy. I was back to square one. On my own on depression island, with a pregnancy to cope with. Once again I'd disappointed my parents. My father was working overseas at the time and his only comment was that I'd taken away the opportunity for them to say how proud they were of me on my upcoming 21st. Now there would be no party – just a baby.'

During this time, if you'd known Yvette she would have looked like just any other 20 year old. If you didn't recognise the signs that suggested bipolar disorder, you'd have put her down as a difficult young woman.

'After a lot of thought and discussion, I decided to keep the baby. I wanted him to feel I was home for him. I wanted this baby to have the opposite experience of my life. I named him Cayden, which means fighter because I wanted him to grow up strong and confident.' As she tells me this her face lights up, as

184

it does throughout the interview every time she mentions her children.

'My boyfriend, who was dependent on other people for income at the time, wasn't really in the picture then, especially as I was living with my parents. They didn't want me to marry him and did their best to keep him away. It was really difficult being in the middle as we were still together throughout my pregnancy. Cayden was born in February and by April I returned with my parents to our hometown of Cape Town. Although it was in my best interest at the time, I felt I wasn't part of any decision making and that I was simply being controlled. I felt I was stuck in a cycle of being dependent but felt I had to take responsibility for my mental health.

'By the time I'd settled in Cape Town my relationship was firmly over but my boyfriend wouldn't accept this and even threatened to kill himself. Luckily I'd had a really easy labour and birth, and from the minute Cayden was put in my arms I was in love with this perfect, beautiful boy. At the same time I felt very emotional but my mother soon put a stop to that, telling me not to cry because the baby would feel it. I held back the tears and focused on Cayden. I knew there and then that this was going to be the most beautiful, perfect experience but I had the feeling that his father wasn't going to be part of it.'

With her parents' support, Yvette enrolled in accounting and business science at UCT. She added more pressure by choosing a double major in auditing and information systems, which she says she really enjoyed. Once again, not one to do anything by halves, she also took on a job at the UCT library. And once again the danger signs were there, but no one saw them.

'This was tough, but luckily my parents helped me to employ a full-time nanny for Cayden. As usual I wasn't satisfied with just studying and working and found myself very involved in student leadership as well as chairing various committees. I ended up working at UCT's Open Education Department and was even sent to England to attend a conference. This meant I didn't get much time with Cayden. I also didn't want to be the disciplinarian, but rather the cool mom.

'Around this time I started going to therapy but each year, almost as though it was written into my diary for August/ September, the wheels would fall off. Somehow I suddenly couldn't function but that didn't stop me carrying on with my hectic schedule. No one really connected the dots and said perhaps you should slow down, relax more – and, more importantly, no one defined what was really wrong with me.' A frustrated sigh escapes as she tells me this.

In cases like Yvette's, intervention by mental health professionals should be ongoing; bipolar disorder is a serious illness.

It was only in her third year, when she kept falling ill from things like stomach flu, that Yvette's GP suggested she might have bipolar disorder. Probably picking up not just on Yvette's love of cramming so much into her life, but also on seeing the notes, poetry and prose she'd written, he told her to see a psychiatrist and show him her writing.

'These should have been loud noises that something was wrong. The psychiatrist looked at all this and said we'd have to be really cautious with such a diagnosis. I agreed but I'd also read enough about bipolar by then to feel strongly that I connected with it. Not in a bad way, but with a huge sense of relief. He advised that I just continue with the therapy, which would support me.

'I felt there needed to be more I could do. When I hit my

next really bad bout of depression I managed to pull myself together enough to arrange an appointment with another psychiatrist at a private hospital, where, 20 minutes into the session, he confirmed that I *definitely* had bipolar disorder. He immediately put me on medication, which he warned me this time around I *must* stay on. At the time I was really grateful to him because I thought at last my feelings, depression, highs and lows had a name. When I looked back I could also see why I got into the type of relationships and sexual partners I'd had.

'That immediate euphoria of having a name for what I had slowly evaporated, and once again the medication made me feel so much better that I felt I'd be fine without it. I realise now that what I needed was support to stay compliant with both the medication and therapy. I'd make appointments to see the doctor and therapist but when it came to the day I just couldn't get out of bed. My now six-year-old son was tasked with bringing me my meds. I felt so guilty but didn't understand why I felt like this. All I knew was once again I'd failed,' recalls Yvette, shaking her head sadly.

'By 2012 I was feeling so much better that once again I took myself off the medication and applied to repeat third year. Naturally, the usual cycle started appearing and I quickly started feeling worse. I persevered and started working on group projects with a new team – always wanting to push myself and do more. Here I was again, back into multiple projects and committee work.

'In March that year I met Darryl Hess, the man who was to become my husband, and by August I found myself pregnant again. Having him by my side, though, made a difference and he really helped in terms of my mental health. One of the first things I told him was that I'd recently received a diagnosis of bipolar so if he wasn't cool with this I'd understand. His response was that although he didn't know anything about it he'd immediately read up on it. He kept his word and finally I had someone to help with my medication. Even though he was living and working in St Helena Bay on the West Coast, he'd drive through to Cape Town every weekend and even after work to give me my medication and see I was all right.

'At the time he was just the rock I needed. We married in December 2012 but by early 2013 I found myself admitted to a Cape Town clinic where once again I was put back on medication, which once again I didn't see as a long-term thing. It was like putting on a plaster but not looking deeply for the source. This pattern of clinic stays and changes of medication went on for the next couple of years. Being pregnant, it was hard to stabilise the medication as I couldn't take it in the first 12 weeks.'

For Darryl, hearing that Yvette had bipolar disorder didn't change how he felt about her but left him with confused emotions. 'I first met Yvette in March 2012, just before she was diagnosed with bipolar disorder. When I first heard the words "bipolar disorder" it was quite a shock, but at the same time I didn't really understand what it meant. The only real explanation I had was that her moods fluctuated between two extremes – either very depressed or a manic high. Even though I had a name for this illness, thinking back I couldn't pinpoint right then what that meant for our relationship.

'It was only a few years later that I could see the different phases of our relationship and marriage where her manic or depressed moods played a role.

'Even though some of my friends couldn't understand why I stayed in this relationship, I never felt like turning and running. Maybe, as Yvette says, I'm a born nurturer. I know I was very concerned about what the bipolar diagnosis meant for Yvette and wanted to understand how I could support her in this journey. In those early days I went with her to a few sessions with a psychiatrist, who explained the importance of the medications he was giving her and how she mustn't deviate from her prescription. At the time I was working in Saldanha Bay but would still manage to drive down on weekends to make sure she was all right and that she was taking her pills.

'At the same time I was doing as much research as I could, just to have some sort of grip on what this illness was and what it meant. This confirmed what the psychiatrist had said – that if she didn't take the pills regularly she could either go up or down.'

It was in this time of her life that Yvette was moving towards an important realisation. 'During my varsity years I'd started writing and blogging, but not just about mental health. When my second son, Alexander, was just three months old I fell pregnant again with my third baby, and this time the pregnancy was very complicated. I'd left my high-powered job in the risk advisory department at a top accounting company, as the travelling was just too much. I was now dealing with a difficult pregnancy, a baby, a six-year-old, a husband and a fairly new marriage, as well as living in my own home for the first time. My mental health was still up and down and this pregnancy was certainly not planned. Again, failure hung over me, and this kicked me even further down.'

It took Gabriel's birth to make Yvette realise, at last, that her only option was to stick to her meds. Even though her moods were steadier, she found that as soon as she brought up certain things with her doctor, he'd increase her dosage. Going from

189

being a busy careerwoman to moving to Saldanha for Darryl's work and becoming a stay-at-home mom and housewife didn't help.

I can see this is hard for Yvette to talk about. I ask her if she doesn't want a break, but she says she's fine – and that she's finding the interview a liberating experience.

'I wasn't engaging in the treatment and never questioned the doctor's decisions. Now I realise you have to understand the full picture and engage with your doctor. Now I felt I didn't need my husband to give me the tablets – I could manage on my own. One horrible side effect of staying on the medication, especially after a baby, was the weight gain, with a side effect from the long-term use of the one drug causing me to get psoriasis all over my scalp, taking away the one thing about myself I loved – my hair.' She smiles as she fluffs up her wonderful head of curls.

'At this point I was just concerned with maintaining my medical regime and making sure I didn't go into psychosis, but felt I didn't need therapy, which I thought was just somewhere to offload. When I felt my mind starting to overwork, I'd simply take more medication, which helped still my mind and sleep but left me drugged and lethargic. Luckily I had domestic help with the boys, but one of the problems with bipolar is hypersensitivity – so just hearing them laughing in the next room was difficult at times. I was stable but I certainly wasn't healthy or engaging in their lives.'

'For a long time I was under the impression that all I had to do is make sure she took her meds and then everything would be fine,' Darryl continues. 'This would ensure she stayed within this narrow band and not go into the extremes of bipolar. I didn't realise it wasn't as easy as that. Many of the meds made her numb emotionally, so it was almost as if whatever problems started creeping up in our marriage we couldn't properly address them.'

By then, though, Darryl had learnt to see the warning signs. 'Normally Yvette would go down before she'd go up and it took a while before she could identify the symptoms herself. I could see it coming when she'd start taking on ten different things simultaneously or would start a project then leave it in the middle to tackle something else – all in the span of three months. Then I knew something wasn't right. She'd always been a very energetic person, doing three jobs at a time, so at first I didn't think much about it, but in time I came to know when things were getting to a dangerous point.

'There were also other signs, such as extreme irritability and being highly sensitive to sound. I felt quite powerless to help her but what I could do was just be there for her, to listen and not judge. I was working a lot of weekends and long hours at the time, which was really hard for me and her.'

Yvette thought she'd found the perfect compromise to soothe herself, one that kept her calm and engaged. She started drinking. What started out as a couple of glasses soon became a bottle; before she knew it, she was hiding empty bottles in cupboards.

'My saving grace was a new friend in the area, who was also a blogger, had worked in the mental health field and was a recovering alcoholic. I asked her if she felt it was normal to hide bottles in a cupboard. She said, "No, it's not normal, but don't worry, we'll chat about it." Shortly after this, she sent me a message saying she wanted to take me to Alcoholics Anonymous [AA]. She'd been in both AA and Narcotics Anonymous [NA] as well as working in a rehab centre. So in 2015 I attended my first AA meeting and early in 2016, after two failed attempts, I managed to stop drinking. My two youngest boys were then three and four.

'Going to AA gave me the same relief I'd found when I was diagnosed with bipolar disorder. And with these people I didn't have to feel ashamed. I understood my drinking was a coping mechanism and an addiction which with some people would translate into eating or excessive gym. From there I just started writing more and more blogs and poetry about my illness and what I'd discovered and was going through. This was an incredibly liberating experience and people would message me saying thank you for writing, sharing this and informing us.'

I ask Darryl if there were ever times he felt like giving up and walking out. Although he's honest about how hard it's been throughout the interview, I can hear his sense of commitment to Yvette and his children. 'Marriage is never easy and has to be worked at, but add in bipolar disorder and you've immediately got more complications,' he says. 'You need to understand and know your partner really well. I'm really lucky that Yvette has done a lot of internal work to understand who she is. She's done so much emotional and mental work which has really helped her a lot.

'There were also times when she was suicidal and had to be admitted to a clinic for a three-week stay. Apart from suddenly having to take over running the house and children, you find yourself having to put your total trust in the nursing staff and mental health professionals. I'd always promise Yvette she'd be okay and I had unwavering faith that, despite things being so hard, you just had to believe everything would be fine and that she'd get through this rough time.'

Yvette proudly tells me how she's now been over two years

sober and that she is sticking to her medication regime. She's also found a great local mental health support structure that has been really good for her.

'Finally finding a great psychiatrist and therapist, and really understanding what my condition was about, changed my life. I also discovered the South African Depression and Anxiety Group who encouraged me to become involved in sharing my experiences and helping others.

'How did these experiences affect my children? Cayden definitely remembers certain things and even now he and my other sons know that when everything becomes too loud for me they need to go and play outside.'

From Darryl's point of view, things are definitely looking up. 'We've come a long way, especially in the last year. We've been able to decide what we want as individuals. Previously it's been the children and the illness first – never us. You can get lost in the illness, which takes complete control of everything, becoming the centrepiece of your life.

'It's also very important as a couple or partnership to be cognisant of bipolar issues. You also have to be able to separate the small stuff. Yvette and I have been fortunate to be able to do that and we can now say to each other, "That's your issue, not mine – I can't fix that." This has taken a long time to work out but it's working for us.

'I think the most important thing I'd tell someone in my position is to do thorough research on your partner's illness, especially the medical side, which I don't think I did that well. It does place a strain on you and at the beginning I started isolating myself. I just wanted to be alone. I was always waiting for the next incident to happen. It couldn't be a positive thing but something bad just waiting to happen.

193

'There were many times I wanted to give up but more often I'd see that glimmer of hope and I knew it was worth fighting for,' he concludes.

For Yvette, the current outlook is positive. 'Right now I'm seeing what is known as a functional doctor,* who has a team who support me using nutrition and lifestyle to monitor my condition. So far, almost for the first time in my life, I feel like myself. I feel empowered, and at the same time if something should go wrong I now know what to do. I know the triggers – talking too fast, and I'll meditate and switch off. I've also learnt mindfulness, which is such a gift. Something so simple and it's free. It takes a while to find out how to be present and accept what you have and incorporate it into your life. I needed the label my condition provided, but that doesn't limit me. I'm still a bit of a people pleaser but now I question whether I'm doing things for the right reasons.

'During one of my clinic stays I started painting, which I found I really loved. They recommended I take this further when I was discharged and this has proven to be a real game changer in my life. I attend classes and with the people I met in art school have formed a collective where I'm using my business knowledge to plan exhibitions and sell our art. And no, I'm not overdoing it. These days I know when to pull the plug. Something that has healed me has now become my career.'

---

* Functional medicine is a systems biology-based approach that focuses on identifying and addressing the root cause of disease. Each symptom or differential diagnosis may be one of many that contribute to an individual's illness.

TOOLBOX TIPS

Level of functioning isn't everything

❏ People who function at a high level (still succeeding at work, for example) may not realise that they need help.

❏ Just because someone 'looks fine', doesn't mean they are. Don't assume someone is okay – ask them how they're doing. Creating space for people to express their feelings is crucial. Waiting for a high achiever to say something is wrong may never happen.

Suicide sensitivity

❏ Describing the act of suicide as *committing* suicide insinuates that the person has done something wrong, like committing a murder. This is stigmatising.

❏ People who engage in suicidal behaviour need help, not more stigma.

Insist on information

❏ The more someone understands why they're taking medication and why they need to be in therapy, the less distressed they feel and the more compliant they'll be.

❏ If you don't understand your diagnosis, what the different medications are for and/or what your treatment options are, you may need to put your foot down and insist on a clear explanation.

Meditation and routine

❑ Meditating, setting goals and establishing routines are all beneficial in the management and promotion of mental health.

❑ Mindfulness doesn't require you to have a completely still mind. It's okay to get distracted. The goal is purely to notice when this happens and gently bring your attention back to the present moment.

Medication

❑ When on psychiatric medication, if you start to feel good that means it's working! Don't adjust your dose or stop taking your medication without consulting a psychiatrist or doctor, as this can disrupt the treatment process.

Teamwork

❑ The treatment process is most effective if it involves working with a psychiatrist, psychologist and support system. Everyone must be accountable; it won't work if you just rely on the doctors. Your commitment to taking your medication, implementing self-care and engaging in a therapy process makes all the difference.

10

ZANE WILSON

Panic disorder

When I first met Zane Wilson, all I'd been told was that she'd started a support group for anxiety and depression. What I didn't know then was how this one interview would change the course of my career in terms of mental health reporting. And it wasn't just me that she had this influence over but countless South African media representatives over the years through SADAG.

This story is so much more than what happened to her as she discovered her panic disorder – it is also about how she relentlessly grew her organisation to impact the lives of so many people.

What hooked me particularly was the energy and passion she had then, in 1995, for talking about her mental health problems and actually wanting publicity for them. This was almost unheard of in those days. Very few publications, or radio or television stations, were running stories about mental health.

That day, sitting in her lounge, Zane explained that her working life up until a few years before her diagnosis had consisted of 15-hour days as the national marketing and sales director for a cosmetics and toiletries company. 'In those days

I was under constant pressure which was fine and I flourished on it. But there came a day when it was obvious I needed a stay in hospital just to regain some strength and repair my nerves. I thought that would do it – a few days' hospital stay resting and I'd be back on track.'

What Zane didn't realise then was that this was just the beginning of a very long road that would take her to hell and back. The first thing they did at the hospital was put Zane on medication to relax her, but this had just the opposite effect.

'Instead of feeling calm I went hot and cold, my palms began to sweat and I started to shake. If someone told me this today, I'd immediately know these were the classic symptoms of a panic attack but then all I knew was that I had to get out of that hospital room.' I was immediately caught up in Zane's story and found it easy to relive those moments with her.

She was in a private room with very large glass windows, which for some reason took on horror proportions to Zane, making her feel like diving right through them to get out. 'Somehow I knew instinctively that the drug they'd given me had brought on this condition. I was too scared to tell the nursing staff in case they put me on a different drug which might make me feel even worse. I took out the drip and the next day, after a sleepless night, discharged myself. Looking back I realise that was irrational but right then it seemed just the right thing to do.'

After this, the attacks started happening two or three times a week until they became almost a daily occurrence. 'I hesitantly went to see a psychologist but she didn't really understand what was happening to me either. At that stage all I could put it down to was that I was "going crazy".'

At this point in my health writing career I knew very little about mental health and would have used words like 'crazy' and 'mad' myself, without thinking about their derogatory nature. As Zane's story unfolded I realised just how much I didn't know about mental health. I wasn't even sure, like many other people, if I knew the difference between a psychiatrist and a psychologist.

Zane continued with her harrowing story. 'I'd be sitting in a boardroom about to present a report or give a presentation when this overwhelming feeling of panic would kick in and I felt like I had to get out of there as quickly as possible. To make things worse I'd just started a sports management company which plunged me into high-powered meetings and running stress-filled events. To help me through these I always made sure I had another staff member with me, night or day, so the minute I felt an attack coming on I could ask for a glass of water or to get a file from my car – just to give me those few minutes of breathing space. It was almost impossible to stay focused on a meeting when I knew that the next attack could see me losing it completely.'

As Zane recalled these meetings, her normally open features clouded over and she drew in her breath as though reliving those awful moments. The attacks would last up to six minutes but having someone with her gave her a feeling of security. The one thing she couldn't bear was the thought of being on her own.

'Organising major sporting events like the Dusi Marathon or rugby cups, which involved a major amount of planning and travelling, was particularly hard. Even when I returned home I always made sure my husband was there waiting.'

For Brian Julius, Zane's husband of 36 years, this has also been a difficult journey, especially in those early days when he didn't know what was wrong with Zane either. He'd married this coordinated, businesslike, functional woman who could work at an international level and fly on her own around the world, but who suddenly couldn't drive around the block.

'There were also the normal day-to-day things like shopping and driving, especially when this involved shopping centres. I managed to get people to give me lifts to and from work and somehow managed to come up with reasons for people to come to the shops or even the hairdresser with me. But there are only so many times you can say you're feeling a bit dizzy or overtired. I once tried shopping on my own and got down one aisle successfully before dropping my shopping and running out the shop half way down the next aisle.

'I'd developed a complete fear of being alone, even for 10 or 15 minutes. The attacks would see me breaking out into a sweat, battling to breathe, with my body shaking and my vision blurring. With my chest tightening it felt like a heart attack.'

This brought Zane's life to a complete halt, and still she had no knowledge of what was happening to her. 'I felt I couldn't tell anyone as again that word "crazy" came to mind as to what they'd think of me. I didn't have a name for what was happening – I just knew I was mentally not well. Somehow I kept going at work. This gave me a reason to get up every day, although once the attacks increased to three or four a day I was forced to seek more real help.'

During the ten years of Zane's illness there were one or two odd years where there was an improvement but an unexpected trip overseas, or too many early mornings and late nights, would send her back to square one. 'I knew there had to be someone out there who would know what was wrong with me, if not in South Africa, then overseas. I started researching bookshops, libraries, searching for anything that would give me a clue to my condition. This of course was way before Google so getting information or finding other people with similar symptoms was almost impossible.

'When we tried to define my condition the best we could come up with was agoraphobia – a fear of being unsafe outside the home – and when I found an article written by an American doctor I immediately wrote to him. He replied with a two-page letter offering me hope and explaining that what I had was an illness, and recommended some reading. I had had no luck in the UK either and, after consulting so many medical experts and trying various medications, which seemed to increase my anxiety, even cognitive behavioural therapy, I was becoming really desperate for an answer.

'This was when I decided to travel overseas for three months on what I thought would be a relaxing holiday, which turned into a nightmare, with my condition becoming so severe that Brian even sent for my mother in the UK to help with me. By then I was in a permanent state of anxiety. I went back to my psychologist who realised I was suicidal.'

For Brian, it wasn't what he'd signed up for. 'When I first met Zane at the end of 1982, she was in the process of setting up a sports management company that would in only a few short years become South Africa's largest sports event company,' he explains. 'It was extremely difficult for me to reconcile this fearless lady who wouldn't hesitate to stand up to some of the most powerful and arrogant team managers and rugby captains, with the woman who was unable to take a step out without being accompanied. Like most people, mental health was to me a complete unknown, depression a figment of one's imagination, with the best way to cope with this being "to just get over it".

201

'When her regular meetings with her psychologist seemed to be a total waste of time, I didn't expect the meeting with Dr Mike Berk to achieve anything different. Only following his diagnosis of panic disorder and the correct prescription, and the almost immediate recovery, did I actually begin to understand the depths of despair and the wasted years of struggling to lead a normal life.'

For Zane, the turning point was meeting the man who would not only diagnose her panic disorder, but help her lay the foundations for what would become SADAG. 'My psychologist, seeing how desperate I was, suggested I see Professor Mike Berk from the Psychology department at Wits University [he is now the Head of Psychiatry at Deakin University in Victoria, Australia]. He diagnosed panic disorder straight away, and as much as I was relieved to know I wasn't going crazy and that my condition did have a name, I also felt enormous frustration at the ten wasted years of my life. Although I resisted at first, we eventually found the right dosage of antidepressants and tranquillisers and within three months I was able to lead a normal life again. I could finally drive around and function normally without fear or needing someone with me all the time.'

Zane now not only knew what was wrong with her but had also put together a small mountain of information about her illness, leading Professor Berk to suggest she start a support group. He agreed that the problem was simply lack of awareness plus the stigma associated with anything related to mental health. Knowing that Zane had a track record of taking unknown ideas and building them to successful businesses, he suggested she turn her talents into creating awareness for panic disorder and its treatment.

So Zane borrowed a room at the Sandton Library, got a small write-up in a local paper and expectantly put out 20 chairs. She was amazed when over 90 people arrived, especially as it was a weekday morning. 'Professor Berk and Dr Frans Korb [now chairman of SADAG's board] were the speakers and I'll never forget the relief on those people's faces to be among others who really understood what they were going through. Treatment options were discussed and solutions clearly explained. We eventually had people sitting in the aisles and standing at the back of the room. This showed us that there was a great need for a group like this.'

Dr Korb clearly recalls that first meeting. 'The room was packed with all kinds of people, from academics, peers from Wits Psychiatry, patients and enthusiasts all keen to get the organisation going. Even though we ran out of chairs, nothing could dampen the expectations of what the meeting intended to do – get SADAG started. After this each meeting grew, over-flowing with attendees, and one meeting especially stands out where, expecting around 30 traditional healers, we found 100 or so arrived eager to hear about the "Western" point of view on mental illness.'

One woman who attended that morning had got her husband to drive her from Witbank and asked if they could run similar groups there. This was the catalyst that drove Zane to take it further. Things started moving very quickly; with people needing to be trained to answer phones and organise talks, they realised they would need money to get a support group, originally called the Panic and Anxiety Group, going properly. Here once again Zane's business background came into play, seeing her lobby pharmaceutical companies who produced panic disorder medications to come on board. It seemed nothing could hold her back.

Psychologist Dr Colinda Linde, now a household name herself in the field of mental health, became involved with Zane at this point in her journey. 'When I first met this tiny firecracker with a melodious voice I soon realised that dynamite does indeed come in small packages. Her determination to spread the word on mental health saw her march into meetings with various pharmaceutical companies to request funding in a way that held no possibility of a no, yet was never rude. And she was only getting started. There's a good reason the private numbers of several captains of industry today appear in Zane's little black book – the one packed full with colour-coded meetings, notes, names and numbers. There's also a good reason why these titans, along with the rest of us, respect and admire her the way we do,' recalls Dr Linde, now a past chairperson and member of SADAG's board.

Before long, Panic and Anxiety Groups were springing up, not just around Johannesburg but countrywide. With Zane's background in marketing and media, it wasn't long before the press heard what she was doing and the interest began, with my feature being her first big magazine story. The media wanted to highlight the severity of such illnesses and the lack of information about them.

Added to this were Zane's recruitment and managerial skills, which saw the project go ahead at double the speed anyone expected. 'In the beginning we had a mornings-only secretary to try and field calls, which were starting to come in non-stop. My phone never stopped ringing, even at midnight.' The group was well on its way to becoming a vital mental health tool in South Africa.

Sponsorship slowly started to come in; as the phones became

busier, two more lines were added, with more staff and the first volunteers being trained. They soon outgrew the small room at Zane's home and moved to an office space in Benmore Gardens. Shortly after this they held a meeting to explain their work to mental health professionals, universities, media and others: what the Panic and Anxiety Group did and how they were helping to lobby for patients' rights.

'We lobbied everyone we could, from government to medical aids and anyone who would listen to us, and those who wouldn't, making sure our voice was heard through various different language media. Our message was simple – we needed the government to work with us and the media to help people understand more about mental health and [patients'] rights.'

As Zane looks back after 26 years, I can see that even she's amazed at how far they've come but still frustrated at how much more she'd like to do. 'One of the biggest drawbacks which kept popping up was the complete lack of help for the black community. There was minimal treatment and no information, talks or support groups, particularly in rural areas. Luckily we got funding to work in townships and over the years have reached so many people in need in rural areas of the country.'

Word started to spread. 'In those early years we travelled all over the country giving talks in towns and townships, talking to police, teachers, municipal workers, social workers, fire departments – anyone who would come to our meetings. We particularly reached out to hospital workers and nurses in emergency rooms who weren't familiar with illnesses such as panic disorder. We often found ourselves in remote areas working 14 hours a day to reach people and help break the stigma of mental health.'

I accompanied Zane and her team on a few of these early trips, which were a mixture of great joy, fun and at times chaos when they ran out of refreshments and chairs for the hordes that would show up. People were desperate for information and it was really rewarding to see how grateful these communities were for this help. Zane and I still chuckle as she reminds me of some of the 'less than two-star' places we found ourselves staying in.

'Occasionally when we thought we wouldn't get a good turnout our driver Thabo, who is still with us 26 years later, would leave home in the early hours of the morning to arrive in time to drive around the area alerting people with a megaphone ahead of the meeting. There were times we were literally overwhelmed with the turnouts where 250 people would arrive, including local government officials. At one time in the Botshabelo Stadium outside Bloemfontein local officials even went out and came back with sandwiches and pies for everyone.

'As we started becoming visible even in remote areas such as the Eastern or Northern Cape, we quickly realised that to make a real impact in the black community we would need to reach out to traditional healers. So in 1996, together with Dr Frans Korb, we decided to hold a meeting in Johannesburg for about 25 traditional healers, mainly from Soweto and Alexandra. Once again the attendance outweighed our seating, with almost 100 traditional healers, many in their full garb, arriving. Dr Korb gave his talk, which was translated, and being careful not to criticise their role in the community but to rather empha-sise the need for them to be informed on mental health, it went down incredibly well.

'They asked us question after question which with the help of the translators we were able to answer. One elderly lady stood up at the end and addressed the crowd who we could see respected and listened to her. She explained, particularly around panic attacks, why they should all consider getting help and training from us.'

Mental health in many black communities is closely linked with the work and culture of traditional healers and through SADAG I've been involved in several stories about this over the years, talking to traditional healers who have taken SADAG's advice and education to heart. As Zane says, this doesn't mean their role is redundant in helping their communities, as the very fact that traditional healers will spend time really listening to people is often very beneficial. But there are still cases where families take their loved ones to often less-than-honest traditional healers where these people will often be chained to walls, locked in dark rooms and even kept as slaves.

Very soon it became clear that the diversity of mental illnesses – panic disorder, bipolar disorder, depression, obsessive compulsive disorder, schizophrenia and so many others – that they were receiving calls about signalled the time for a name change for the organisation. And so SADAG was born. Zane proudly explains, 'This was the start of the South African Depression and Anxiety Group and now not only were we dealing with people suffering from mental health issues, we were working with many psychiatrists, psychologists, GPs and other specialists.'

She concludes, 'SADAG continues to grow due to the incredible staff and team we have, all fighting for patients' care, education, treatment, rights and support. We need to constantly grow, whether doing talks for 100 patients, or 100 doctors, a magazine for professionals [*Mental Health Matters*], over 30 000 newsletters monthly, a counselling container in large townships like Diepsloot, help lines for corporations, lobbying for medication rights, supporting press, and opening more and more support groups in urban and rural areas. As we have more commitment from the professionals and gradually from the government, we'll become more visible, more helpful, and continue to grow at a rapid speed.'

Zane's recognition for her work in mental health awareness and support::
- ❏ South African Woman of the Year for Health (1998)
- ❏ World Health Organization (2003)
- ❏ Federation of Mental Health (2003)
- ❏ World Bank Marketplace (2003)
- ❏ Finalist – Pan African Health Awards (2006)
- ❏ Recognised as one of the Top Influential Leaders in Health Care in South Africa by the South African Institute of Health Care Managers (2011)
- ❏ South African Selection Board Chairman for Rosalynn Carter Fellowships for Mental Health Journalism (2004)
- ❏ Order of the Baobab (2012)

SADAG's work has been endorsed by the World Bank, the Department of Health, the Department of Education, Johns Hopkins, the US Embassy, De Beers, the World Federation for Mental Health, the World Health Organization, the European Union, the Department of Social Development and the Global Fund.

11

CHARLENE SUNKEL

Schizophrenia

My knowledge of schizophrenia was so limited when I first started writing on mental health that I thought it was the end point of a progression from depression to bipolar. This, along with the idea that someone with schizophrenia has a split personality, is a common misperception. Depression and bipolar are mood disorders, but schizophrenia is when someone has lasting psychotic symptoms (hallucinations and/or delusions). Not everyone with schizophrenia has auditory or visual hallucinations, however. Some have what are called gustatory delusions – imagined tastes.

Early in my mental health writing journey, I was sent to Soweto to write a story about a young man with schizophrenia who was on medication and living in a care facility. I'm not sure what I expected that day, but it wasn't the happy, energised young man I met. My perceptions had been coloured by my research, which told me how people heard voices and saw things that weren't there. There was a part of me that was a little nervous about this encounter.

There's something about the word 'schizophrenic' that does that.

Now, many years later when I arrive to meet Charlene

Sunkel, my understanding of schizophrenia is a lot different. The warm, friendly voice that buzzes me in to her apartment tells me she is certainly doing well these days.

I first heard of Charlene in February 2020 while I was attending a conference about the stigma surrounding mental health in Nairobi, Kenya. When people heard I was from South Africa, they said, 'But you must know Charlene Sunkel.' To their amazement, I didn't – but after hearing people from all around Africa, the USA and the UK raving about the wonderful work that Charlene does around the world, I made a point of finding out more. Charlene started the Global Mental Health Peer Network, '[t]he platform for people with lived experience with mental health conditions to share journeys, experiences, perspectives, views and opinions … embracing our humanity, appreciating our diversity and uniting our voices towards achieving our common goals'. When I returned from Kenya I managed to connect with Charlene, and was thrilled when she agreed to share her remarkable story, which gives a real insight into life with schizophrenia.

At her door, I'm met by the loud squawks of her two birds, a parrot and a parakeet, competing about who could make the most noise. 'Sorry about them,' she laughs as she lets me in.

As I sit down, her phone rings. I assure her that it's no problem if she takes the call, but she switches off the phone – which, she tells me, rings non-stop. From what I've heard of her and her work, I can believe it. Of course, I also know that this wasn't always the case for 48-year-old Charlene. She appears to be supremely confident. Is this the real Charlene, I wonder, given how much she's been through? Or is it something she's practised to get by?

Today, her work sees her travelling the world, serving on numerous international boards, committees and organisations to which she takes her passion for spreading the word about not only her journey, but also what others with mental illness go through, to help break the pervasive stigma.

Twenty-two years ago Charlene, diagnosed with paranoid schizophrenia and locked up in a mental institution from hell, wasn't sure she'd ever have a life again.

It all started with a big life change. Growing up in Piet Retief, a small Mpumalanga town, Charlene felt safe surrounded by her parents and two sisters. But her life changed dramatically at the sensitive age of 11 when the person she most adored, her mother, fell ill and died. 'This had a big impact on me, and when my father remarried a year later it wasn't easy. Suddenly from always being the good child I became a rebel, not sure if this was with or without a cause. At just 12 years old I started smoking and drinking. Doing everything I wasn't supposed to do, particularly in the tight-knit Afrikaans community we lived in.

'In high school I made sure I did just enough work to scrape through each year, and when we moved to Pretoria as a result of my dad getting a big promotion I suddenly found myself in Grade 11 in a much larger high school. I really struggled at first, but actually started liking it towards the end of my school years. What I didn't like was my home life, so instead of study-ing further after matric I made up my mind that as soon as I could I'd get a job and move out of the house. I was quite lucky and found a job in health administration, the idea being that I'd study while I was working. I thought I might study towards working with animals, or even architecture.'

At 18 years old, with the court agreeing to declare her an adult, Charlene bought her first flat and thought, *This is it – my life's perfect*. But just a few months into her acclaimed inde-pendence, things started to go wrong. With the words 'mental health' never featuring in her or her family's vocabulary, no one saw the signs. It was just Charlene being a difficult teenager.

'The first signs were a complete switch from being an outgoing party girl to suddenly becoming completely withdrawn. Where I'd been very social, I now didn't want to leave my flat. My biggest problem became looking people in the eye.'

One of the most common symptoms of paranoid schizophrenia, along with hearing voices or sound effects, is paranoid delusions. For Charlene, this was very real. These types of behaviour changes can also be a warning sign for other mental health issues, but either way they need to be taken notice of and checked as early as possible.

'Things would get stuck in my head and I'd make a big thing of it – one relating to the saying that the eyes are the windows to the soul. In my mind, this meant if I look someone in the eye, they're going to steal my soul. This was the first sign of my paranoia.'

The hard part for people with schizophrenia is that not only do they get laughed at if they tell anyone about what they're seeing or hearing, but that, for them, nothing could be more real than the delusions they're experiencing. Schizophrenia is a real illness, with delusions and paranoia being symptoms. When you see that homeless person walking around, shouting and talking to themselves, they could well fit this profile.

But with no knowledge of schizophrenia or its symptoms, Charlene didn't see this as paranoia and her illness just became worse. Paranoia can take many forms, from seeing others as being 'out to get you' to feeling that you have some grand religious calling. In the schizophrenic person's mind, these are very real and drive his or her days. When this was happening to Charlene 22 years ago, very little about mental health was written about in the media or featured on radio or television.

'Slowly, my life started changing. With strange thought processes whirling through my mind I'd completely lose track of time. My work colleagues couldn't help but notice the change in me. From always being the first at work I'd constantly arrive late. Even though I was getting up at the same time, I'd get caught up listening to the voices in my head and before I knew it, it was 9 am and I hadn't left home yet. Sometimes on my way to work I'd forget where I was going and even had to pull off the road to think about it for a few minutes. Needless to say, my work deteriorated – and as my boss was also a medical doctor, she encouraged me to seek help.'

Charlene put off seeing a psychiatrist as she feared being labelled 'crazy'. 'I couldn't live with that. Even though my colleagues and other people were nagging me to go, I resisted. Living on my own meant I could hide a lot, particularly from my family. But eventually even they realised things were going badly wrong. I'd be invited to my dad's place for a braai, arrive, get out of the car and walk through the house without greeting anyone, turn around, get into my car and go home.

'I knew I had to see someone and as I was 18 I went to an adolescent psychiatrist, who referred me to another one when I turned 19 a month later. All he did was prescribe medication, which he sternly told me to take without explaining what it was or why I had to take it. When I asked, "What's wrong with me?" he kept avoiding the question. He didn't want to tell me anything.' In Charlene's case this was almost a criminal omission: without proper information, how could she start healing?

All mental healthcare service users today have a right to clear information and an explanation of their diagnosis. If they don't receive this, they must ask. This is where it really helps if a family member or someone they trust can go with them when they meet medical professionals.

'This led to my condition getting even worse. Did he think I was intellectually incapable of understanding what he would tell me, or that I wouldn't be able to interpret the information? By then I'd already lost control and was getting worse. I decided to see another psychiatrist and this time he gave me the diagnosis of paranoid schizophrenia.'

Charlene had never heard the term before. Before 2013, paranoid schizophrenia was seen as a 'subtype' of schizophrenia, but today this label is no longer used. In 1991, without Google around, there was very little information available about mental health. 'In those days the only thing related to mental health I'd ever heard was when people would talk in hushed tones about someone having a nervous breakdown. I didn't even know what that was. In my mind it was someone physically collapsing – as in breaking down. I'd certainly never heard the word "schizophrenia".'

As she relates her story, I feel the pain coming through in her words. She's told it over and over, but it never gets any easier to say, 'I have schizophrenia.'

'My go-to place for information was the library, so in my lunch hour I'd find a quiet corner where I could sit without anyone seeing which books I was looking at, trying to identify my symptoms. What was awful to read was that this condition had a poor prognosis, with no way of ever regaining my life back. This really hit me hard. But I finally knew what was wrong with me, which in part was a relief, as if it wasn't a real illness it would have meant I had a weakness. What made things harder was that I had no one to share this with. I was too scared to tell anyone.

214

'Instead of feeling better, the side effects of the medication made me feel horrible, and instead of trying to adjust my medications the psychiatrist simply said, 'You must take them.' I felt like telling *him* to take them and then tell me if he could tolerate the side effects. In fact, it would be another nine years, trying every medication you could think of with nothing working, before they found the right medication, which I've been on ever since.'

It can take a long time, persistence and patience to find the right meds – and to find a psychiatrist who really listens to you and gains your trust. Managing the medication for a person with schizophrenia is particularly complicated; they need help.

The next nine years were sheer hell for Charlene. With all the negativity she felt from every quarter, she started spiralling downwards. When she mentioned to her family that a psychiatrist wanted to talk to them about her illness, it made things even worse.

'While they were blaming themselves for what happened to me, they also said I was obviously involved in Satanism, and sent a family member to the hospital to bring me a book on the subject. I was furious. Then they said I must be on drugs, which again was utter rubbish. Somehow they needed to put my illness in a box, with someone or something to blame.'

Denial can be the go-to place for families when confronted with such illnesses. They want to distance themselves from attaching mental illness to one of their own. These are words to whisper in the privacy of your own home; heaven forbid anyone should ever find out.

There are so many different factors that can cause such illnesses – genetic predisposition, upbringing and trauma, to name a few – that it's hard to pinpoint their cause. Blaming or stigmatising the person with the illness doesn't help; what he or she desperately needs is support.

'By 1994 I was spending more time in than out of hospital, eventually seeing me medically boarded in 1997. My employer had been very patient, even though they had wanted to board me before then. This wasn't surprising, as there were times I'd arrive at work thinking I was properly dressed but was in my pyjamas and slippers. When I looked in the mirror, instead of brushing my hair, whatever bits were sticking up I'd just take the scissors and chop off. I hate to think what people who shared my bus ride to work thought. Instances like this ultimately led my employers to call someone to fetch me and take me straight to hospital. I'd really wanted to hang on to my job, not only for the independence but a reason to get up in the morning. Losing my job meant losing my flat, my car – everything. All I had left was one suitcase with my meagre possessions in it.'

One of the first signs of many mental illnesses is losing interest in how you look and your hygiene practices. Charlene thought she didn't look abnormal – she thought she was fine. Of course, she wasn't.

'Now it was back and forth to the hospital, sometimes voluntarily and other times being forcibly admitted. In my mind this was what I imagined prison to be like – hearing the sounds of large keys turning in locks as you're confined. And the treatment, well there was only one word for it – appalling abuse!' Her expression tells me how difficult these recollections are, but there's also a lot of anger in her voice and body as she recalls the worst period of her life – anger that has led her to fight against involuntary admissions and to improve the desperate conditions in psychiatric hospitals.

I can also hear the frustration in her voice when she talks

216

about the response she gets when she raises the issue of the condition of these hospitals – that there is a 'lack of funding'. 'When I think of those bare, dirty walls and torn couches, I have to wonder – how much does a pot of paint cost, or a couple of plants? Dig some up from the gardens if you have to and use some of the incredible creativity of the patients to do some artwork for the walls. This would cost nothing. It was a very hostile environment. Research shows that where an effort has been made to make the physical environment better, there's been a reduction in admissions, and shorter stays, which in the end would save the government money.'

But her terror continued. After a hospital stay in 1994, where once again Charlene was locked up, the social worker contacted her family to say she could leave the hospital but couldn't live on her own as she couldn't do anything for herself. They found what was called a psychosocial rehabilitation centre – a type of halfway house – for her. Even though they supervised her medication there, she still had a number of relapses.

'I saw psychologists, but being the stubborn person I am and not the type to "share" easily, this had no effect. Looking back I wonder if maybe the medications would have helped if I'd had family or peer support. The system was relying on us popping pills to magically make us better.

'Inevitably in 1998 I ended back in lock-up. That day I'd gone to an outpatient facility to see a psychiatrist and get my medication before going back to the rehab centre. Obviously they sensed I wasn't doing so well but instead of telling me what was happening they kept saying I must wait as the doctor wanted to see me again. It got to 5 pm, when they were supposed to close, and I started getting suspicious and angry. Before I knew it they'd injected me with a sedative and I was on my way back to yet another psychiatric institution. To this day, I still don't know why. All I remember is being taken to the lock-up ward by a nurse whose name I'll never forget.

'They take all your clothes and possessions, everything, away from you and give you horrible hospital clothes. Then, in the passage on the way to the dormitory, this nurse turned to me and said, "I hate people like you. I suggest you don't fall asleep because I plan to come in the night and hang you by your sheets in the bathroom and once you're dead I'll call the ambulance and say you committed suicide!" Obviously I couldn't fall asleep after that. I was frightened to death that she'd carry out her threat. This was the worst experience of my life!'

As Charlene tells me this shocking part of her story, I see her shrink into herself at the memory, and shudder with her at the thought of how such treatment would make me feel. It sounds like a scene from the movie *One Flew Over the Cuckoo's Nest*. Conditions are generally better now, but people shouldn't be afraid to complain – complaints do get addressed, and doing so is an important step in improving these services.

'The whole experience there was dreadful, the treatment, the food and the most excruciating humiliation of my entire life – the baths, or rather, bath. One bath for 40 women. At 7 am we'd line up and troop to the bathroom where *one* bath filled with a small amount of warm water awaited us. You stood naked in the queue and then along with one or two other women at a time got thrust into the bath. They handed you slivers of soap and squirted what felt like dishwashing liquid on your hair while you tried your best to clean yourself. Obviously the worst punishment was to be at the end of the line and have to get in to the filthy cold water. I worked out a sure method

218

to make it to the top of the queue – cigarette bribery. These women would do anything to get their hands on cigarettes, so these became my currency to be the first in the bath.

'There were four or five toothbrushes for everyone to use and you dared not complain as you'd be beaten up, pushed, screamed and sworn at. Once your ablutions were over, they'd hand you clothes and you went to the dining hall for breakfast before being locked up again, this time in a long room with concrete floors. You've now had your medication and all you wanted to do was sleep but the only place to do this was on the cold concrete floor. When you tried to tell anyone outside about your treatment the staff denied it, saying you can't believe someone like that – they're lying.'

Charlene pauses, takes a deep breath and then steels herself to continue her story. 'If they felt you'd misbehaved, then there was the towel treatment. They wet a towel, put it around your neck and twisted it until it became tighter and tighter and finally unbearable. This firmly fell under human-rights abuse. I regularly saw patients being physically abused and I tried complaining to the doctor. The nurses again would say these patients were psychotic or that the patient harmed themselves – this while the nurse's hand mark was clearly shown on the patient's face. The patients rarely complained, fearing victimisation.'

I've heard such stories often; the problem is finding people brave enough to speak out. If they do, they have to admit that they were once a patient.

'I'm not sure what it's like today but I believe they have cameras in the wards and hopefully it's improved. As bad as it was, this diabolical treatment led to my career today, particularly when everyone continually told me I'd never go anywhere or achieve anything. I thought, *Who are you to tell me that?* Just having those thoughts was part of my healing. Don't tell me I'll never live on my own, go anywhere alone, drive a car again or manage my own finances. I quickly realised there was no one to help me and if I was going to get out of there and on my feet again it was up to me to make it happen. I couldn't believe these nurses and staff could get away with what they were doing. It was so wrong morally and ethically, and I knew I had to try and help make a difference. The only way I could do that was by getting myself on the right track and out of there.'

By the time Charlene was able to get discharged, she was – in her words – 'still a bit of a mess', but determined to come right. At first, she would sleep for most of the day, only getting up to go to the toilet or to eat or drink something.

'When I left hospital I was taken back to the rehab centre, where I told them I was leaving that very same day. They weren't happy, but there was nothing they could do to stop me. So I called someone to come and get me, and with the pension money I'd luckily got from my previous job I rented a flat, and bought a computer and some software. Then the work on myself began. Each day I set my alarm for 7 am, dragged myself out of bed and into the bath. Sheer torture at the time but I knew I had no other option. Then I'd go walking, first just two blocks and increasing it weekly to three blocks and more until I got physically stronger. I'd buy a newspaper to read rather than a book, as my concentration was too poor to read more than a couple of articles at a time.

'Being a creative person, I was happy to get back into writing poetry, which started to wake up my mind. Some days I'd do washing but each day had to be structured. I'd organise my day as though I was working, with a lunch break and knock-off time. I forced myself into this schedule for four months and although it was incredibly difficult it became routine.'

The power of self-care, routine, goal setting and exercise should never be underestimated. It's within anyone's control, with or without a mental illness, and can be a significant factor in the effectiveness of treatment. Many people with mental illnesses struggle to find and establish structure for themselves, which is why they could really benefit from seeing an occupational therapist or psychologist.

When life is tough, there comes a moment when you say, 'So much and no more'. For Charlene, this moment had arrived. She was determined never to look back. Looking around her tastefully furnished, very neat apartment, it's hard to imagine the Charlene that once was.

'One morning I woke up and thought, *This is it – I'm ready*. Although I was still on medication, I took it in the evening so being sleepy wouldn't be a problem. I started teaching myself graphic design and also placed advertisements at local university campuses offering to type theses. I offered to do business cards and posters for people and organisations. Suddenly I had a purpose and was earning money.'

This makes a huge difference to self-esteem. Even doing menial tasks can significantly improve overall functioning and everyday life. Society needs to give more people like this a chance.

'Then I started volunteering in the mental health field, joined a support group and became their secretary which I really enjoyed. I thought back to all the people I'd met in hospital and at rehab who were so creative in the visual and literary arts and thought how sad that their work gets locked inside an institution and no one gets to see it. If people could see this work they'd change their perceptions that people with mental

221

health conditions were useless. But how could I do this? So I spoke to the organisation that ran the rehab home, pitching the idea of starting a magazine where we could publish this artwork, short stories and poetry. To my joy they agreed, and we produced the magazine *Walk My Way*, published quarterly.

Charlene was back in the world of work. 'At the magazine's launch in 2005 I told my story and was approached by a woman from another disability organisation asking, Why not write a play to raise awareness? At the time I'd never even seen a theatre play, let alone written one. But I thought, *What could I lose?* So I researched how to go about this, looked at script samples, sat down and wrote a play on schizophrenia, which I went on to produce and ran until just a few years ago.'

In 2006, Charlene was offered a full-time position by a provincial organisation as their awareness and advocacy officer, a position tailor-made for her. Although her family and some friends told her she wouldn't last, she grabbed the job with both hands.

'I started working there from Mondays to Thursdays not to tire myself too much, but found I was so bored on Fridays I asked if I could do a full week. I worked there for over eight years and started an extremely successful movement around people's lived experiences. This really helped my reputation and the word spread on the type of work I was doing.'

In just eight years, Charlene wrote two more plays – one on bipolar disorder, showing the role African culture plays in these illnesses, and another on depression. By showing the play on schizophrenia to medical students, she hoped to encourage them to go into psychiatry – not always the most attractive field to medical students. Everything she did had one common goal: breaking down the stigma of these illnesses.

'We ended up combining my story with schizophrenia and the bipolar play to make a short feature film (now on YouTube), *Two Beds Madness Revealed*. To get really good publicity, we used known South African actors who worked at a reduced fee.' (To view the film, go to https://www.youtube.com/watch?v=IUOyluXGJu4.)

'I used to talk about my story at corporate wellness days and it was interesting to see people's reactions. One day, at a banking organisation, one of the staff asked what I was going to talk about and I said schizophrenia. Her response was, "Oh, people who commit crimes and murder people." I didn't reply, choosing to stay quiet instead.

'My presentation explained the different mental health disorders and then I said, "I have schizophrenia." Their mouths collectively dropped open. After the session I couldn't believe how many of them swarmed around me, as they either had someone in the family or knew someone who suffered from a mental health condition and wanted to share these stories, sometimes wanting advice.

'When I appeared on a television talk show a caller phoned in to say it didn't *look* as though I had schizophrenia. How should I look? This tells you a lot about people's perceptions. I had a similar reaction on radio when someone phoned in to say it didn't *sound* as though I had schizophrenia. Another interesting reaction was the shock when people discovered I'd travelled overseas on my own.'

Sadly, it is a common misconception that people with illnesses like schizophrenia are violent. There are just as many people who are violent and commit crimes, and who aren't mentally ill. Before you label someone, find out more about the illness.

Schizophrenia isn't something that goes away with a course

of medication. It is something that Charlene will have to live with for the rest of her life. Perhaps the memories of what her life was like have made her determined to manage this illness as best she can.

Her best friends, who live close by, are watchful. If they receive strange WhatsApp messages, or hear something different in her voice, or see something in her look, alarm bells ring and they spring into action.

'A sure sign, I've been told, is that my eyes go dead. My friends have the contact number for my psychiatrist and permission to call her. Initially I was going to government clinics but the trouble there is inconsistency with the doctors you see, which stops you building what is a very important relationship with your treating psychiatrist. You mostly see interns and if they think you look slightly down they'll just increase your medication, not bothering to ask if anything had happened or why you were feeling this way. Not once did they suggest I take a day off to chill, but rather automatically changed my medication. Now I go the private route and for the last three years I've been seeing the same psychiatrist who knows exactly how to manage me and my medication without any hospitalisation.'

It makes a huge difference to have continuity of care, as psychiatric history plays a vital role in the treatment process. If the doctor doesn't have all your information, your treatment won't be as effective. But this means that if you don't have medical aid or access to a government hospital with a good psychiatric unit, you are likely to have less success in treating an illness like this.

For Charlene, employment is central to self-esteem. 'The most important thing for me is the structure my work provides. My job gives me purpose, which is vital. I advocate a lot about the importance of employment. I advise people that if they can't get work, to start out by volunteering to prove themselves. People will see that physically and mentally they can do the job and it's a way of getting a foot in the door.'

One thing Charlene is certain of is that for people with mental health issues – especially schizophrenia – applying for jobs at large companies and corporates is still almost impossible.

'We asked fourth-year medical students, after they watched one of our plays, whether they'd let someone with schizophrenia look after their child if they had one. "No" was their instant response. This from people with a medical background. So the reality remains, people won't employ someone with schizophrenia. Even me, with all my achievements and awards, if I went for a corporate job and disclosed my condition, would they offer me a job? Probably not.'

Recognition came in other ways for Charlene, though. In 2010 she was contacted by Professor Vikram Patel, a world-renowned and highly respected figure in global mental health. He'd heard about her and invited her to lecture at his Leadership in Mental Health Course in India.

'My first thought was, *Are you serious? You think I can lecture psychiatrists on mental health?* But again I had nothing to lose and when you've lost everything you can take chances. So I went and, along with people from Africa, India and Nepal, shared my perceptions and opinions, which went really well.'

From there, Professor Patel invited Charlene to be part of the EMPOWER Project as a communications consultant, helping people develop materials as she'd done to help raise awareness in their countries – many of whom were far worse off than South Africans.

Charlene's voice takes on a note of pride as she tells me

225

about the many boards and committees she serves on, both here and overseas. I can tell that she feeds off the energy that this overload of work gives her.

'In 2018 I resigned from my job to work full-time running my Global Mental Health Peer Network as its founder/ CEO. I managed to get funding and finally put my plans into action. From the people with lived experiences I'd met over the last few years, I knew the needs in this field, especially in low- and middle-income countries where political factors still deprive people of their basic human rights. With this ingrained stigma, people are often afraid to talk about their mental health problems, and so never achieve recovery and take on leadership roles.'

Charlene has grown her organisation. Today, it operates in 21 countries and is still growing; she hopes to get all her representatives to work at a global level.

'Right now I'm in a really good place. Running the Global Mental Health Peer Network has not only given me a life purpose, but makes a valuable contribution to society and changes people's lives. Now I don't see my journey as just being an evil part of my past, but rather that I've used that negative experience to positively change things. I had to go through the nightmare of incarceration at those dreadful hospitals to become a part of changing things.

'My life is better now than it's ever been – I've got good relationships with my family, who are proud of my work, although sadly my father died before he could see my achievements. He died thinking I was a lost soul. Today my family ask me about mental health issues and have learnt a lot themselves. Only in recent years have I really shared my experiences with them and realised they didn't know what I went through. I also have very close and caring friends who add to my life. I'm not saying I'm cured – that's not an option and I still have a lot to do on myself. If I don't stick to my medication regime things go horribly wrong quite quickly, but these days I'm aware of this and the importance of rest and a balanced life.'

The more you support people with mental illness, the more they can achieve. Expecting someone to fail can be a far bigger hurdle than the illness itself.

As we come to the end of our time together, I can see the toll that recounting this story has taken on Charlene, but I can also see the passion for her work shining through.

'Where I am today is down to the people who gave me opportunities, who believed in my abilities rather than focusing on what I couldn't do. I owe them a huge debt of gratitude because without them I'm not sure I'd even be here. One of my key messages is for people to believe in their own abilities. It's so easy to transfer other people's negativities onto yourself. If I keep telling you you're useless, you can't do anything, you're going to believe it and start behaving that way. Never accept this. The only person who knows you is you. The only person who can build your future is you. Even though you may have struggles with certain symptoms, you can still find a way to live with them and manoeuvre around them. Having a purpose – and hopefully employment – is so important.

'A mental health diagnosis doesn't have to be the end of the road. Just like having diabetes or heart disease, you find a way to live with it. The difference is with those illnesses people can still find employment. The only way we can change people's attitudes to mental health is by speaking out and showing that our contribution to society is as important as anyone else's. Give people – all people – a chance.'

TOOLBOX TIPS

Crazy, psycho, mad versus sick, in need of help

❏ Schizophrenia is wildly misunderstood and stigmatised. To stop perpetuating the stigma, educate yourself before expressing an opinion about the illness.

❏ People with schizophrenia experience psychotic symptoms that disturb their thoughts and perceptions, resulting in difficulties in understanding what is and isn't real.

❏ Psychotic symptoms include hallucinations, delusions (false beliefs), incoherent speech and behaviour that's inappropriate for the situation.

❏ Someone who is psychotic may seem crazy, but it's important to remember that these are symptoms of a severe illness – which is nothing to laugh at, mock or demean.

Know your rights

❏ Everyone has a right to a clear explanation of his or her diagnosis. If you don't receive this, insist on it. Knowing your diagnosis can help to understand why you're experiencing what you are and is a good reminder that you're not alone.

❏ If you're struggling to understand, attend the session with someone you trust.

Patience, persistence and continuity of care

❏ It can take time to find the right combination and

dosage of medications, with difficult side effects along the way.

❑ Making your own decisions about your medication when you get tired or frustrated isn't a good idea and can significantly delay the entire process, resulting in added, unwanted admissions. Be patient and persistent.

❑ Try to find a psychiatrist you trust and who can continue to see you throughout the treatment process, as continuity of care is very helpful.

Don't underestimate people

❑ Believing someone can't do something without giving him or her the chance to try or supporting him or her along the way is incredibly limiting. Trying to change people's expectations that you'll fail can be a far bigger hurdle to overcome than the symptoms of your illness, which you can learn to manage.

❑ Our society is ableist, placing focus on what someone can't do. If we focus on what someone *can* do, even if in a limited capacity, it can be empowering and life-changing.

❑ Having a purpose is crucial to our self-esteem. It may take extra effort to support people with certain mental health difficulties, but it could make all the difference to them.

Creating structure and routine

❑ It's not always easy to establish structure and routine, but it is important. If you need help, seek assistance from an occupational therapist or a psychologist.

Acknowledgements

Firstly and most importantly I want to thank my incredible colleagues and friends at SADAG (South African Depression and Anxiety Group), particularly CEO and founder Zane Wilson and Operational Director Cassey Chambers, whose help in all matters mental health is invaluable.

As I was completing this book, Covid-19 came into our lives and complicated things immeasurably and for this reason I particularly want to thank my publisher Louise Grantham and her great team at Bookstorm for their guidance and encouragement to bring this book to fruition.

I must also give a big thank you to Cipla for believing in the importance of this book and sponsoring its publication. They do so much for mental health in this country that it's a privilege to be associated with them.

This book wouldn't exist, of course, without all the very brave people featured in these pages who not only generously gave of their time to talk to me, but who bared their hearts and souls in the telling of their stories. Thank you.

Finally, to my daughter Alexa Scher, who through my involvement with SADAG and mental illness over the last 26 years had no choice but to become a clinical psychologist. As well as writing many of the tips at the end of each chapter, she was a constant sounding board and guiding light throughout this journey.

Cipla

DEPRESSION
SHOULDN'T BE
A LABEL

DEPRESSION IS WHAT I HAVE NOT WHO I AM

Call the Cipla **SADAG 24-hour
mental health helpline** on **0800 456 789**
or via **WhatsApp on 076 882 2775**
between 9am – 5pm.

THE SOUTH AFRICAN
DEPRESSION AND ANXIETY GROUP

CIPLA MEDPRO (PTY) LTD. Co. Reg. No. 1995/004182/07. Building 9, Parc du Cap, Mispel Street, Bellville, 7530, RSA.
Website: www.cipla.co.za Customer Care: 080 222 6662. [567014434]